Python for Beginners

Coding, Programming, and Web-Programming Made Simple and Fast. Become a Python Programmer (2022 Guide)

Vere Hunt

Table of Contents

Chapter 1

Basics Of Pythong Programming

Python For Beginners

Welcome! Is it true that you are totally new to programming? In the event that not, at that point we assume you will be searching for data regarding why and how to begin with Python. Luckily an accomplished software engineer in any programming language (whatever it might be) can get Python rapidly. It's likewise simple for apprentices to utilize and adapt, so hop in!

Introducing

Introducing Python is commonly simple, and these days numerous Linux and UNIX circulations incorporate an ongoing Python. Indeed, even a few Windows PCs (strikingly those from HP) presently accompany Python previously introduced. On the off chance that you do need to introduce Python and aren't certain about the errand you can locate a couple of notes on the BeginnersGuide/Download wiki page, however establishment is unremarkable on most stages.

Learning

Before beginning, you might need to discover which IDEs and content tools are custom fitted to make Python altering simple, peruse the rundown of initial books, or see code tests that you may discover supportive.

There is a rundown of instructional exercises appropriate for experienced software engineers on the BeginnersGuide/Tutorials page. There is likewise a rundown of assets in different dialects which may be helpful if English isn't your first language.

The online documentation is your first port of call for authoritative data. There is a genuinely short instructional exercise that gives you essential data about the language and kicks you off. You can pursue this by taking a gander at the library reference for a full depiction of Python's numerous libraries and the language reference for a total (however to some degree dry) clarification of Python's linguistic structure. On the off chance that you are searching for basic Python plans and examples, you can peruse the ActiveState Python Cookbook

On the off chance that you need to know whether a specific application, or a library with specific usefulness, is accessible in Python there are various potential wellsprings of data. The Python site gives a Python Package Index (otherwise called the Cheese Shop, a reference to the Monty Python content of that name). There is additionally a quest page for various wellsprings of Python-related data. Bombing that, simply Google for an expression including the word "python" and you may well get the outcome you need. When in doubt, ask on the python newsgroup and there's a decent possibility somebody will put you in good shape.

Installation of Phyton

You might need to print these guidelines before continuing, with the goal that you can allude to them while downloading and introducing Python. Or then again, simply keep this archive in your program. You should peruse each progression totally before playing out the activity that it depicts.

This archive shows downloading and introducing Python 3.7.4 on Windows 10 in Summer 2019. You ought to download and introduce the most recent form of Python.

The present most recent (as of Summer 2019) is Python 3.7.4.

Recall that you should introduce Java, Python, and Eclipse as each of the 64-piece applications.

Python: Version 3.7.4

The Python download requires around 25 Mb of plate space; keep it on your machine, in the event that you have to re-introduce Python. When introduced, Python requires about an extra 90 Mb of circle space.

Downloading

Snap Python Download.

The accompanying page will show up in your program.

Snap the Windows interface (two lines beneath the
Download Python 3.7.4 catch). The accompanying page
will show up in your program.

Snap on the Download Windows x86-64 executable
installer connect under the upper left Stable Releases.

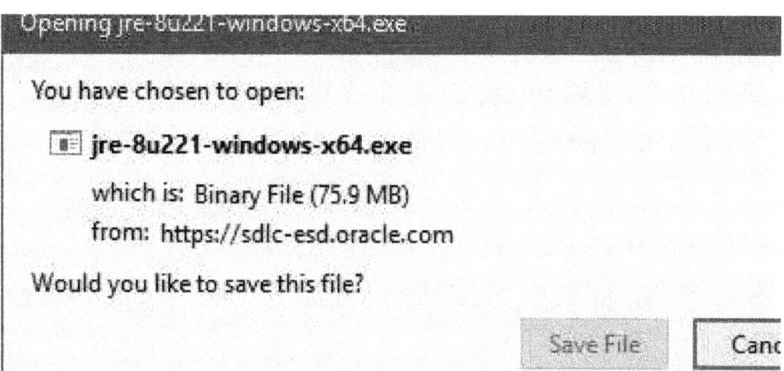

The accompanying spring up window titled Opening python-3.74-amd64.exe will show up.

Snap the Save File button.

The record named python-3.7.4-amd64.exe should begin downloading into your standard download organizer. This record is around 30 Mb so it may require a significant stretch of time to download completely on the off chance that you are on a moderate web association (it took me around 10 seconds over a link modem).

The document ought to show up as

Move this record to a progressively perpetual area, so you can introduce Python (and reinstall it effectively later, if essential).

Don't hesitate to investigate this page further; in the event that you need to simply proceed with the establishment, you can end the tab perusing this website page.

Start the Installing guidelines straightforwardly underneath.

Introducing

Double tap the symbol marking the document python-3.7.4-amd64.exe.

A Python 3.7.4 (64-piece) Setup spring up window will show up.

Guarantee that the Install launcher for all clients (suggested) and the Add Python 3.7 to PATH checkboxes at the base are checked.

In the event that the Python Installer finds a prior adaptation of Python introduced on your PC, the Install Now message may rather show up as Upgrade Now (and the checkboxes won't show up).

Feature the Install Now (or Upgrade Now) message, and afterward click it.

At the point when run, a User Account Control spring up window may show up on your screen. I couldn't catch its picture, however it asks, Do you need to permit this application to make changes to your gadget.

Snap the Yes button.

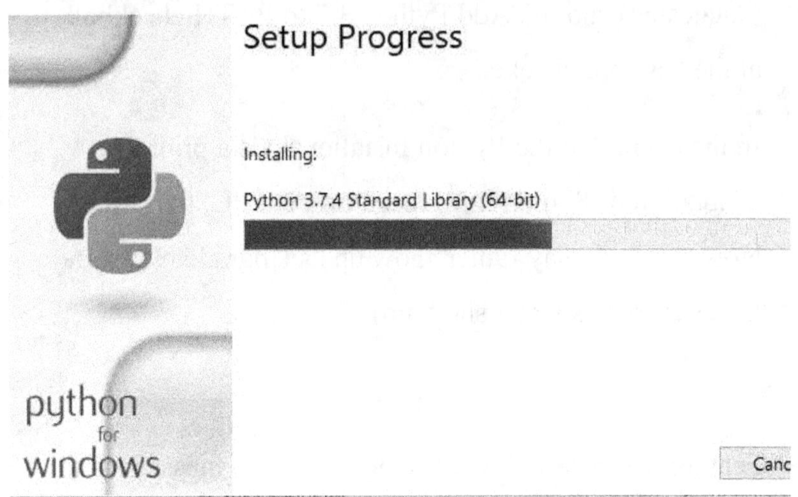

Another Python 3.7.4 (64-piece) Setup spring up window will show up with a Setup Progress message and an advancement bar.

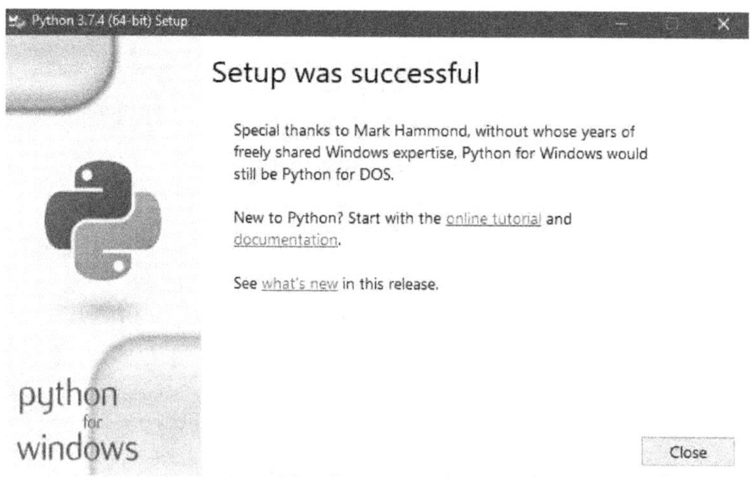

During establishment, it will show the different segments it is introducing and move the advancement bar towards consummation. Before long, another Python 3.7.4 (64-piece) Setup spring up window will show up with a Setup was successfuly message.

Snap the Close catch.

Python should now be introduced.

Checking

To attempt to check establishment,

Explore to the registry

C:\Users\Pattis\AppData\Local\Programs\Python\Python37

(or to whatever index Python was introduced: see the
spring up window for Installing stage 3).

Double tap the symbol/document python.exe.

The accompanying spring up window will show up.

A spring up window with the title
C:\Users\Pattis\AppData\Local\Programs\Python\Python37
\python.exe shows up, and inside the window; on the
principal line is the content Python 3.7.4 ... (notice that it
ought to likewise say 64 piece). Inside the window, at the
base left, is the brief >>>: type exit() to this brief and press
enter to end Python.

You should keep the record python-3.7.4.exe some place on your PC on the off chance that you have to reinstall Python (not likely essential).

You may now adhere to the directions to download and introduce Java (you ought to have just introduced Java, however in the event that you haven't, it is OK to do so presently, inasmuch as you introduce both Python and Java before you introduce Eclipse), and afterward adheres to the guidance to download and introduce the Eclipse IDE. Note: you have to download/introduce Java regardless of whether you are utilizing Eclipse just for Python)

Installation of Phyton in Macintosh Operating System

As a flat out fledgling to programming, you can rapidly figure out how to do bunches of cool things utilizing only your Python mediator and basic Python contents. Nonetheless, you're going to need a couple of more apparatuses in the long run to assist you with growing to increasingly complex activities. Why not get acquainted with them now?

For me, the hardest thing about spreading out was making sense of what devices I truly required and how to decipher their introduce directions. Here's a rundown of instruments you will require and a rundown of simple strides to pursue to get set up on a Mac. I'll clarify what each line of code is doing so you can become familiar with a tad about working with an order line interface all the while. The entirety of this should deal with Mac OS X 10.7 and 10.8.

1. Introduce XCODE

Xcode is Apple's Integrated Development Environment (IDE), and there are a few apparatuses that accompany it that we'll require later. You can get Xcode in the Apple appstore. It's a really huge download, however this is the least demanding approach to get these apparatuses on your machine. In the event that you get exhausted while you're pausing, you could skirt ahead and do stages 2, 5, and 6 at this point. On the off chance that you need an elective method to simply get the instruments you need, without the entire IDE, look here.

Once Xcode is introduced, despite everything you have to introduce the Apple direction line apparatuses! They're anything but difficult to get, however. Under the Xcode menu, click inclinations. On the window that springs up, go to the Downloads tab. Discover "direction lines devices" and snap the introduce button.

2. OPEN TERMINAL. GET COMFY.

In the event that you've never utilized Terminal or some sort of direction line interface previously, it's a smart thought to pause for a moment to acquaint yourself with how they work. Here's a speedy introduction. Later you can get familiar with more with the free online book, Learn Command Line Interface the Hard Way.

I like to have a focal spot to store the entirety of my programming ventures, so I have an organizer in my home catalog called Code. To make another organizer called Code, open up Terminal. You ought to be in your home catalog. Just to ensure you could type the accompanying in your Terminal window. Try not to type the $, however.

Direction line guidelines for the most part start with $, which speaks as far as possible of your brief. The brief is the series of characters Terminal prints out to tell you it's prepared to acknowledge directions. The compact disc implies change registry. In the event that you don't determine where to go, it sends you to your home index. Presently, to make an envelope called Code, you would type:

The mkdir part signifies 'make index'. A registry is closely resembling what Finder calls envelopes. On the off chance that you make a registry through your direction line, it will appear as an organizer in Finder. The Code part is a contention for this direction. mkdir needs us to indicate a string that will be the name of the new registry, so we pass it the Code contention. In contrast to album, mkdir will give us a blunder on the off chance that we don't likewise give a name. As demonstrated as follows, the mistake message (second line) reveals to us that we utilized mkdir wrong and gives us some direction on the best way to utilize it. Anything in sections is discretionary, yet the registry name isn't!

3. Introduce HOMEBREW

Homebrew is a bundle administrator for OS X. A bundle is an assortment of code records that work together. Introducing them for the most part implies running a content (a touch of code) that places certain records in the different indexes. A ton of the bundles you will need will have conditions. That implies they expect you to have different bundles previously introduced on your PC. Homebrew will discover and introduce conditions for you AND it will keep them sorted out in one area AND it can reveal to you when updates are accessible for them. Over the entirety of that it gives very accommodating guidelines when everything doesn't go easily. You can peruse increasingly about it at Homebrew's site. For the time being, introduce Homebrew utilizing the accompanying line of code:

So what's happening here? The last piece is clearly a URL. If you somehow happened to open this URL in your program, you would simply observe code. This is a Ruby content that guides your PC to introduce Homebrew. The twist part is an order line device that moves documents utilizing URLs. The - fsSL part is a mix of four choice banners for twist that determine how to deal with the record at the url. In the event that you need to find out about what these banners do, type man twist at your direction brief. (You can utilize man before most directions to open up a manual page for that order.) We additionally need to really execute this Ruby content, so we utilized the order ruby toward the start. The - e is an alternative banner for ruby that executes a string as one line of code, for this situation, the "$(curl â€¦/go)" part. You may need to adhere to a couple of more guidelines to complete the introduce, yet Homebrew will assist you with doing as such.

4. Introduce PYTHON

Python accompanies OS X, so you can presumably don't have to do this progression. You can check this by composing python - rendition into Terminal. In the event that you get a mistake message, you have to introduce Python. In the event that Terminal prints something like Python 2.7.3 where the definite numbers you see might be extraordinary, you're good to go to proceed onward to step #5.

On the off chance that for reasons unknown you don't have Python or on the off chance that you need to get the present form, you would now be able to do this effectively with Homebrew! Whenever you use Homebrew, you will begin your direction with blend pursued by the Homebrew order you need to utilize. To introduce the most recent form of python 2, just type:

On the off chance that you'd preferably introduce the most recent variant of python 3, supplant python with python3.

5. Introduce PIP

There are a couple of bundle administrators that are explicit to Python, and pip is the favored one. The name pip means "pip introduces bundles". pip has one dependeny- - disseminate, however Homebrew doesn't have the foggiest idea how to introduce it is possible that one. Fortunately, both disseminate and pip can be effectively introduced with python contents that are accessible on the web. We can utilize twist, much the same as we did to get Homebrew.

This time we are getting and executing each content in two directions, where we did it across the board order previously. Recollect that you can look into what - O does with $ man twist, in case you're interested.

It's conceivable that you will run into an authorization issue here. Each record on your PC stores data about who can get to and adjust it. The get-pip.py content is going to attempt to compose records to a portion of your framework registries and it's conceivable that your client account doesn't have the correct consents. You can get around that however. On the off chance that you get a blunder for one of these Python directions about authorizations, type sudo before the remainder of the order. Sudo means "superuser do". The superuser has consent to change framework records and when you state sudo, you are going about as the superuser. You will require the administrator secret word to do this.

For more data about utilizing pip, you can go here.

6. Introduce VIRTUALENV

A virtual situation is helpful when you begin to get invovled with ventures that have unique or clashing conditions that you dont need to introduce all inclusive on your machine. For instance, you may utilize a library that requires Python 3 and have another task that is just perfect with Python 2.

To introduce virtualenv, just:

7. Introduce GIT AND MAKE A GITHUB ACCOUNT

Git is a form control framework. It monitors the modifications you make to your code and different records related with a task, without putting away numerous duplicates of each document. It will likewise assist you with consolidating your work with that of different developers in case you're dealing with a communitarian venture. To introduce Git, type the accompanying at your direction brief.

Github is a site that utilizations git and is the most well-known way individuals share their code. You can utilize it only to back up your own undertakings or to have a brought together store for a cooperative venture, but on the other hand it's kind of an internet based life site for software engineers. You can take a gander at others' code, pursue ventures you're keen on, submit bugs, and even contibute code to open source ventures. On the off chance that you need to engage with an open source undertaking or discover great example code, Github is the most ideal approach to do it. Go to github.com and adhere to the guidelines to make your record.

In case you're a little confounded about this progression, or need to know why and how you should utilize Github, you should understand this.

8. WHAT NOW?

You have a ton of useful assets on your machine, presently and it might be a touch of overpowering. That is alright, you don't need to learn them at the same time, however at any rate you have them set up now. however, there are additionally a lot of assets unreservedly accessible on the web to enable you to learn. Take a stab at perusing the Pyladies Resources page, or simply utilizing Google to discover what you need. Chatting with a progressively experienced developer is constantly useful too. Have a ton of fun!

Installation of Phyton in Windows Operating System

Python 3 Installation and Setup Guide

Chapter by chapter guide

Windows

Stage 1: Download the Python 3 Installer

Stage 2: Run the Installer

Windows Subsystem for Linux (WSL)

Linux

Ubuntu

Linux Mint

Debian

openSUSE

CentOS

Fedora

Curve Linux

Assembling Python From Source

macOS/Mac OS X

Stage 1: Install Homebrew (Part 1)

Stage 2: Install Homebrew (Part 2)

Stage 3: Install Python

To begin working with Python 3, you'll have to approach the Python mediator. There are a few regular approaches to **achieve this:**

Python can be acquired from the Python Software Foundation site at python.org. Normally, that includes downloading the fitting installer for your working framework and running it on your machine.

Some working frameworks, outstandingly Linux, give a bundle supervisor that can be rushed to introduce Python.

On macOS, the most ideal approach to introduce Python 3 includes introducing a bundle director called Homebrew. You'll perceive how to do this in the applicable area in the instructional exercise.

On versatile working frameworks like Android and iOS, you can introduce applications that give a Python programming condition. This can be an incredible method to rehearse your coding aptitudes in a hurry.

On the other hand, there are a few sites that enable you to get to a Python mediator online without introducing anything on your PC by any means.

Note: There is an opportunity that Python may have been transported with your working framework and is as of now introduced. Regardless of whether that is the situation, it might be that the introduced form is obsolete, in which case you will need to get the most recent form at any rate.

In this Python establishment control, you'll see bit by bit how to set up a functioning Python 3 conveyance on Windows, macOS, Linux, iOS, and Android. So how about we begin!

Windows

It is profoundly improbable that your Windows framework transported with Python previously introduced. Windows frameworks ordinarily don't. Luckily, introducing doesn't include considerably more than downloading the Python installer from the python.org site and running it. How about we investigate how to introduce Python 3 on Windows:

Stage 1: Download the Python 3 Installer

Open a program window and explore to the Download page for Windows at python.org.

Underneath the heading at the top that says Python Releases for Windows, click on the connection for the Latest Python 3 Release - Python 3.x.x. (As of this composition, the most recent is Python 3.6.5.)

Look to the base and choose either Windows x86-64 executable installer for 64-piece or Windows x86 executable installer for 32-piece. (See beneath.)

For Windows, you can pick either the 32-piece or 64-piece installer. This is what the distinction between the two **comes down to:**

In the event that your framework has a 32-piece processor, at that point you ought to pick the 32-piece installer.

On a 64-piece framework, either installer will really work for most purposes. The 32-piece rendition will commonly utilize less memory, however the 64-piece adaptation performs better for applications with serious calculation.

In case you're uncertain which adaptation to pick, go with the 64-piece variant.

Note: Remember that on the off chance that you get this decision "wrong" and might want to change to another rendition of Python, you can just uninstall Python and afterward re-introduce it by downloading another installer from python.org.

Stage 2: Run the Installer

When you have picked and downloaded an installer, essentially show it to double tapping on the downloaded record. An exchange ought to give the idea that looks something like this:

Windows establishment exchange

Significant: You need to make certain to check the crate that says Add Python 3.x to PATH as appeared to guarantee that the translator will be set in your execution way.

At that point simply click Install Now. It's as simple as that. A couple of moments later you ought to have a working Python 3 establishment on your framework.

Windows Subsystem for Linux (WSL)

On the off chance that you are running Windows 10 Creators or Anniversary Update, you really have another alternative for introducing Python. These forms of Windows 10 incorporate an element called the Windows Subsystem for Linux, which enables you to run a Linux situation legitimately in Windows, unmodified and without the overhead of a virtual machine.

For more data, see the Windows Subsystem for Linux Documentation article on the Microsoft site.

For guidelines on the best way to empower the subsystem in Windows 10 and introduce a Linux dissemination, see the Windows 10 Installation Guide.

You can likewise look at this introduction on YouTube by Sarah Cooley, one of the individuals from the WSL improvement group.

When you have introduced your preferred Linux appropriation, you can introduce Python 3 from a Bash comfort window, similarly as you would on the off chance that you were running that Linux dispersion locally. (See underneath.)

Linux

There is a generally excellent possibility your Linux conveyance has Python introduced as of now, however it presumably won't be the most recent adaptation, and it might be Python 2 rather than Python 3.

To discover what version(s) you have, open a terminal window and attempt the accompanying directions:

python - adaptation

python2 - adaptation

python3 - form

At least one of these directions ought to react with a form, as underneath:

$ python3 - variant

Python 3.6.5

On the off chance that the form demonstrated is Python 2.x.x or a variant of Python 3 that isn't the most recent (3.6.5 as of this composition), at that point you will need to introduce the most recent rendition. The strategy for doing this will rely upon the Linux dispersion you are running.

Note that it is every now and again simpler to utilize an apparatus called pyenv to deal with different Python forms on Linux. To get familiar with it, see our article here.

Expel promotions

Ubuntu

Contingent upon the adaptation of the Ubuntu dissemination you run, the Python introduce guidelines differ. You can decide your neighborhood Ubuntu form by running the accompanying direction:

No LSB modules are accessible.

Merchant ID: Ubuntu

Depiction: Ubuntu 16.04.4 LTS

Discharge: 16.04

Codename: xenial

Contingent upon the rendition number you see under Release in the support yield, adhere to the guidelines **beneath:**

Ubuntu 17.10, Ubuntu 18.04 (or more) accompany Python 3.6 of course. You ought to have the option to summon it with the direction python3.

Ubuntu 16.10 and 17.04 don't accompany Python 3.6 of course, yet it is in the Universe vault. You ought to have the option to introduce it with the accompanying directions:

You would then be able to summon it with the order python3.6.

On the off chance that you are utilizing Ubuntu 14.04 or 16.04, Python 3.6 isn't in the Universe storehouse, and you have to get it from a Personal Package Archive (PPA). For instance, to introduce Python from the "deadsnakes" PPA, do the accompanying:

$ sudo include adept storehouse ppa:deadsnakes/ppa

$ sudo adept get update

$ sudo adept get introduce python3.6

As above, conjure with the order python3.6.

Linux Mint

Mint and Ubuntu utilize a similar bundle the board framework, which much of the time makes life simpler. You can adhere to the directions above for Ubuntu 14.04. The "deadsnakes" PPA works with Mint.

Debian

We discovered sources that demonstrated that the Ubuntu 16.10 technique would work for Debian, however we never found a way to get it to chip away at Debian 9. Rather, we wound up making Python from source as recorded beneath.

One issue with Debian, in any case, is that it for the most part doesn't introduce the sudo order naturally. To introduce it, you'll have to do the accompanying before you do the Compiling Python From Source guidelines underneath:

$ su

$ able get introduce sudo

$ vi/and so forth/sudoers

From that point forward, open the/and so on/sudoers document utilizing the sudo vim order (or your preferred content tool.) Add the accompanying line of content as far as possible of the record, supplanting your_username with your genuine username:

We found a few locales portraying how to get zypper to introduce the most recent variant of Python, yet they appeared to be dangerous or obsolete. We didn't figure out how to get any of them to work effectively, so we fell back to building Python from source. To do that, you should introduce the improvement apparatuses, which should be possible in YaST (through the menus) or by utilizing zypper:

$ sudu zypper introduce - t design devel_C_C++

This progression took some time and included the establishment of 154 bundles, yet once it was finished, we had the option to manufacture the source as appeared in the Compiling Python From Source area above.

CentOS

The IUS Community makes a pleasant showing of giving more current adaptations of programming to "Big business Linux" distros (for example Red Hat Enterprise and

CentOS). You can utilize their work to assist you with introducing Python 3.

To introduce, you should initially refresh your framework with the yum bundle administrator:

$ sudo yum update

$ sudo yum introduce yum-utils

You would then be able to introduce the CentOS IUS bundle which will get you fully informed regarding their site:

$ sudo yum introduce https://centos7.iuscommunity.org/ius-release.rpm

At last you would then be able to introduce Python and Pip:

$ sudo yum introduce python36u

$ sudo yum introduce python36u-pip

On account of Jani Karhunen for his fantastic writeup for CentOS 7.

Evacuate promotions

Fedora

Fedora has a guide to change to Python 3 as the default Python distributed here. It shows that the present rendition and the following barely any variants will all ship with Python 2 as the default, however Python 3 will be introduced. In the event that the python3 introduced on your adaptation isn't 3.6, you can utilize the accompanying order to introduce it:

Curve Linux

Curve Linux is genuinely forceful about staying aware of Python discharges.

Ways of Running Phyton

One of the most significant abilities you have to work as a Python engineer is to have the option to run Python contents and code. This will be the main path for you to know whether your code fills in as you arranged. It's even the main method for knowing whether your code works by any stretch of the imagination!

This bit by bit instructional exercise will control you through a progression of approaches to run Python contents, contingent upon your condition, stage, needs, and abilities as a software engineer.

You'll have the chance to figure out how to run Python contents by utilizing:

The working framework direction line or terminal

The Python intuitive mode

The IDE or content tool you like best

The record director of your framework, by double tapping on the symbol of your content

Along these lines, you'll get the information and aptitudes you'll have to make your advancement cycle progressively beneficial and adaptable.

Free Bonus: Click here to gain admittance to a part from Python Tricks: The Book that gives you Python's prescribed procedures with straightforward models you can apply immediately to compose increasingly lovely + Pythonic code.

Evacuate advertisements

Contents versus Modules

In figuring, the word content is utilized to allude to a document containing a consistent arrangement of requests or a cluster handling record. This is normally a basic program, put away in a plain book document.

Contents are constantly prepared by some sort of translator, which is liable for executing each order successively.

A plain book document containing Python code that is proposed to be straightforwardly executed by the client is typically called content, which is a casual term that implies top-level program record.

Then again, a plain book record, which contains Python code that is intended to be imported and utilized from another Python document, is called module.

Along these lines, the primary contrast between a module and a content is that modules are intended to be imported, while contents are made to be legitimately executed.

In either case, the significant thing is to realize how to run the Python code you compose into your modules and contents.

What's the Python Interpreter?

Python is a great programming language that enables you to be beneficial in a wide assortment of fields.

Python is likewise a bit of programming called a translator. The translator is the program you'll have to run Python code and contents. Actually, the translator is a layer of programming that works between your program and your PC equipment to get your code running.

Contingent upon the Python usage you use, the translator can be:

A program written in C, as CPython, which is the center usage of the language

A program written in Java, as Jython

A program written in Python itself, as PyPy

A program actualized in .NET, as IronPython

Whatever structure the mediator takes, the code you compose will consistently be controlled by this program. Accordingly, the primary condition to have the option to run Python contents is to have the translator accurately introduced on your framework.

The mediator can run Python code in two unique manners:

As a content or module

As a bit of code composed into an intelligent session

The most effective method to Run Python Code Interactively

A broadly utilized approach to run Python code is through an intuitive session. To begin a Python intelligent session, simply open a direction line or terminal and afterward type in python, or python3 relying upon your Python establishment, and afterward hit Enter.

Here's a case of how to do this on Linux:

$ python3

Python 3.6.7 (default, Oct 22 2018, 11:32:17)

[GCC 8.2.0] on linux

Type "help", "copyright", "credits" or "permit" for more data.

>>>

The standard brief for the intuitive mode is >>>, so when you see these characters, you'll realize you are in.

Presently, you can compose and run Python code as you wish, with the main disadvantage being that when you close the session, your code will be no more.

At the point when you work intelligently, every articulation and proclamation you type in is assessed and executed right away:

```
>>> print('Hello World!')
```

Hi World!

```
>>> 2 + 5
```

7

```
>>> print('Welcome to Real Python!')
```

Welcome to Real Python!

An intelligent session will enable you to test each bit of code you compose, which makes it an amazing advancement apparatus and a great spot to try different things with the language and test Python code on the fly.

To exit intuitive mode, you can utilize one of the accompanying alternatives:

stop() or leave(), which are worked in capacities

The Ctrl+Z and Enter key mix on Windows, or only Ctrl+D on Unix-like frameworks

Note: The main dependable guideline to recall when utilizing Python is that on the off chance that you're in question about what a bit of Python code does, at that point dispatch an intelligent session and give it a shot to perceive what occurs.

On the off chance that you've never worked with the direction line or terminal, at that point you can attempt this:

On Windows, the order line is typically known as direction brief or MS-DOS comfort, and it is a program called cmd.exe. The way to this program can differ altogether starting with one framework form then onto the next.

A brisk method to gain admittance to it is by squeezing the Win+R key mix, which will take you to the Run exchange. When you're there, type in cmd and press Enter.

On GNU/Linux (and different Unixes), there are a few applications that give you access to the framework direction line. The absolute most famous are xterm, Gnome Terminal, and Konsole. These are apparatuses that run a shell or terminal like Bash, ksh, csh, etc.

For this situation, the way to these applications is considerably more differed and relies upon the dispersion and even on the work area condition you use. Thus, you'll have to peruse your framework documentation.

On Mac OS X, you can get to the framework terminal from Applications → Utilities → Terminal.

Evacuate advertisements

How Does the Interpreter Run Python Scripts?

At the point when you attempt to run Python contents, a multi-step process starts. In this procedure the mediator will:

Procedure the announcements of your content in a successive style

Arrange the source code to a middle of the road position known as bytecode

This bytecode is an interpretation of the code into a lower-level language that is stage autonomous. Its motivation is to enhance code execution. Along these lines, whenever the mediator runs your code, it'll sidestep this accumulation step.

Carefully, this code streamlining is just for modules (imported documents), not for executable contents.

Ship off the code for execution

Now, something known as a Python Virtual Machine (PVM) comes vigorously. The PVM is the runtime motor of Python. It is a cycle that repeats over the directions of your bytecode to show them coordinated.

The PVM isn't a segregated segment of Python. It's simply part of the Python framework you've introduced on your machine. In fact, the PVM is the last advance of what is known as the Python mediator.

The entire procedure to run Python contents is known as the Python Execution Model.

Note: This portrayal of the Python Execution Model relates profoundly usage of the language, that is, CPython. As this isn't a language prerequisite, it might be dependent upon future changes.

Step by step instructions to Run Python Scripts Using the **Command-Line**

A Python intuitive session will enable you to compose a ton of lines of code, however once you close the session, you lose all that you've composed. That is the reason the standard method for composing Python programs is by utilizing plain content records. By show, those documents will utilize the .py expansion. (On Windows frameworks the expansion can likewise be .pyw.)

Python code documents can be made with any plain content manager. In the event that you are new to Python programming, you can attempt Sublime Text, which is an incredible and simple to-utilize supervisor, however you can utilize any manager you like.

To continue pushing ahead in this instructional exercise, you'll have to make a test content. Open your preferred content tool and compose the accompanying code:

```
#!/usr/container/env python3
```

```
print('Hello World!')
```

Spare the document in your working index with the name hello.py. With the test content prepared, you can keep perusing.

Utilizing the python Command

To run Python contents with the python order, you have to open a direction line and type in the word python, or python3 on the off chance that you have the two adaptations, trailed by the way to your content, much the same as this:

In the case of everything works alright, after you press Enter, you'll see the expression Hello World! on your screen. That is it! You've quite recently run your first Python content!

On the off chance that this doesn't work right, perhaps you'll have to check your framework PATH, your Python establishment, the manner in which you made the hello.py content, where you spared it, etc.

This is the most fundamental and pragmatic approach to run Python contents.

Diverting the Output

Now and then it's valuable to spare the yield of a content for later investigation. Here's the manner by which you can do that:

This activity diverts the yield of your content to output.txt, instead of to the standard framework yield (stdout). The procedure is generally known as stream redirection and is accessible on the two Windows and Unix-like frameworks.

In the event that output.txt doesn't exist, at that point it's naturally made. Then again, on the off chance that the record as of now exists, at that point its substance will be supplanted with the new yield.

The integrated Development Environment

Composing Python utilizing IDLE or the Python Shell is extraordinary for straightforward things, yet those devices rapidly transform bigger programming ventures into disappointing pits of hopelessness. Utilizing an IDE, or even only a decent devoted code proofreader, makes coding fun—however which one is best for you?

Dread not, Gentle Reader! We are here to help clarify and demystify the horde of decisions accessible to you. We can't pick what works best for you and your procedure, however we can clarify the upsides and downsides of each and assist you with settling on an educated choice.

To make things simpler, we'll break our rundown into two general classes of instruments: the ones assembled only for Python advancement and the ones worked for general improvement that you can use for Python. We'll get out some Whys and Why Nots for each. In conclusion, none of these alternatives are fundamentally unrelated, so you can give them a shot alone with next to no punishment.

What Are IDEs and Code Editors?

An IDE (or Integrated Development Environment) is a program committed to programming advancement. As the name suggests, IDEs incorporate a few apparatuses explicitly intended for programming advancement. These instruments generally include:

A manager intended to deal with code (with, for instance, sentence structure featuring and auto-finish)

Assemble, execution, and troubleshooting devices

Some type of source control

Most IDEs bolster a wide range of programming dialects and contain a lot more highlights. They can, in this manner, be enormous and set aside some effort to download and introduce. You may likewise require propelled information to utilize them appropriately.

Interestingly, a committed code manager can be as basic as a content tool with sentence structure featuring and code organizing abilities. Most great code editors can execute code and control a debugger. The absolute best ones interface with source control frameworks too. Contrasted with an IDE, a great committed code manager is normally littler and snappier, however regularly less element rich.

Prerequisites for a Good Python Coding Environment

So what things do we truly require in a coding domain? Highlight records change from application to application, yet there are a center arrangement of highlights that makes coding simpler:

Spare and reload code records

On the off chance that an IDE or editorial manager won't let you spare your work and revive everything later, in a similar state it was in when you left, it's very little of an IDE.

Run code from inside the earth

Additionally, on the off chance that you need to drop out of the proofreader to run your Python code, at that point it's very little in excess of a basic content manager.

Investigating support

Having the option to step through your code as it runs is a center element of all IDEs and most great code editors.

Linguistic structure featuring

Having the option to rapidly spot catchphrases, factors, and images in your code makes perusing and understanding code a lot simpler.

Programmed code designing

Any manager or IDE deserving at least some respect will perceive the colon toward the finish of some time or for proclamation, and realize the following line ought to be indented.

Obviously, there are heaps of different highlights you may need, similar to source code control, an expansion model, form and test apparatuses, language help, etc. However, the above rundown is the thing that I'd see as "center highlights" that a decent altering condition should bolster.

In view of these highlights, we should investigate some broadly useful apparatuses we can use for Python advancement.

General Editors and IDEs with Python Support

Overshadowing + PyDev

Class: IDE

Site: www.eclipse.org

Python apparatuses: PyDev, www.pydev.org

In the event that you've invested any measure of energy in the open-source network, you've caught wind of Eclipse. Accessible for Linux, Windows, and OS X at, Eclipse is the true open-source IDE for Java improvement. It has a rich commercial center of expansions and additional items, which makes Eclipse helpful for a wide scope of improvement exercises.

One such expansion is PyDev, which empowers Python troubleshooting, code fruition, and an intuitive Python support. Introducing PyDev into Eclipse is simple: from Eclipse, select Help, Eclipse Marketplace, at that point look for PyDev. Snap Install and restart Eclipse if fundamental.

Overshadowing with PyDev introduced

Masters: If you've just got Eclipse introduced, including PyDev will be speedier and simpler. PyDev is truly available for the accomplished Eclipse engineer.

Cons: If you're simply beginning with Python, or with programming advancement when all is said in done, Eclipse can be a great deal to deal with. Recollect when I said IDEs are bigger and require more information to utilize appropriately? Overshadowing is all that and a pack of (micro)chips.

Grand Text

Classification: Code Editor

Site: http://www.sublimetext.com

Composed by a Google engineer with a fantasy for a superior content tool, Sublime Text is an amazingly famous code supervisor. Bolstered on all stages, Sublime Text has worked in help for Python code altering and a rich arrangement of expansions (called bundles) that expand the punctuation and altering highlights.

Introducing extra Python bundles can be dubious: all Sublime Text bundles are written in Python itself, and introducing network bundles regularly expects you to execute Python contents legitimately in Sublime Text.

Brilliant Text code supervisor

Masters: Sublime Text has an extraordinary following in the network. As a code supervisor, alone, Sublime Text is quick, little, and all around bolstered.

Cons: Sublime Text isn't free, in spite of the fact that you can utilize the assessment rendition for an inconclusive timeframe. Introducing augmentations can be precarious, and there's no immediate help for executing or investigating code from inside the supervisor.

To capitalize on your Sublime Text arrangement, read our Python + Sublime Text arrangement manage and consider our top to bottom video course that tells you the best way to make a viable Python improvement arrangement with Sublime Text 3.

Evacuate advertisements

Iota

Classification: Code Editor

Site: https://atom.io/

Accessible on all stages, Atom is charged as the "hackable content manager for the 21st Century." With a smooth interface, document framework program, and commercial center for expansions, open-source Atom is constructed utilizing Electron, a system for making work area applications utilizing JavaScript, HTML, and CSS. Python language support is given by an expansion that can introduced when Atom is running.

Iota code manager

Aces: It has expansive help on all stages, on account of Electron. Iota is little, so it downloads and stacks quick.

Cons: Build and troubleshooting bolster aren't implicit however are network given additional items. Since Atom is based on Electron, it's continually running in a JavaScript procedure and not as a local application.

Your First Program in Pythons

How to Get Started With Python?

In this instructional exercise, you will figure out how to introduce and run Python on your PC. When we do that, we will likewise compose our first Python program.

Python is a cross-stage programming language, which means, it runs on various stages like Windows, MacOS, Linux and has even been ported to the Java and .NET virtual machines. It is free and open source.

Despite the fact that the vast majority of the present Linux and Mac have Python preinstalled in it, the form may be obsolete. In this way, it is constantly a smart thought to introduce the most present adaptation.

The Easiest Way to Run Python

The most straightforward approach to run Python is by utilizing Thonny IDE.

The Thonny IDE accompanies the most recent form of Python packaged in it. So you don't need to introduce Python independently.

Pursue the accompanying strides to run Python on your PC.

Run the installer to introduce Thonny on your PC.

Go to File > New. At that point spare the record with .py augmentation. For instance, hello.py, example.py and so forth.

You can give any name to the record. Be that as it may, the record name should end with .py

Compose Python code in the document and spare it.

Run Python on your PC

At that point Go to Run > Run current content or essentially click F5 to run it.

Introduce Python Separately

On the off chance that you would prefer not to utilize Thonny, here's the way you can introduce and run Python on your PC.

Download the most recent variant of Python.

Run the installer record and pursue the means to introduce Python

During the introduce procedure, check Add Python to condition factors. This will add Python to condition factors and you can run Python from any piece of the PC.

Additionally, you can pick the way where Python is introduced.

Introduce Python on your PC

When you finish the establishment procedure, you can run Python.

1. Run Python in Immediate mode

When Python is introduced, composing python in the direction line will conjure the mediator in prompt mode. We can straightforwardly type in Python code and press enter to get the yield.

Take a stab at composing in 1 + 1 and press enter. We get 2 as the yield. This brief can be utilized as a number cruncher. To leave this mode type quit() and press enter.

Run Python in Immediate mode

2. Run Python in the Integrated Development Environment (IDE)

We can utilize any word processing programming to compose a Python content document.

We simply need to spare it with the .py augmentation. Be that as it may, utilizing an IDE can make our life much simpler. IDE is a bit of programming that gives valuable highlights like code indicating, linguistic structure featuring and checking, record travelers and so forth to the software engineer for application advancement.

Coincidentally, when you introduce Python, an IDE named IDLE is likewise introduced. You can utilize it to run Python on your PC. It's a not too bad IDE for learners.

At the point when you open IDLE, an intuitive Python Shell is opened.

Python IDLE

Presently you can make another record and spare it with .py expansion. For instance, hello.py

Compose Python code in the document, spare it. To run the record go to Run > Run Module or basically click F5.

Run Python program in IDLE

Your first Python Program

Since we have Python ready for action, we can compose our first Python program.

We should make an extremely basic program called "Hi World!". A "Welcome, World!" is a basic program that yields Hello, World! on the screen. Since it's a basic program, it's frequently used to acquaint another programming language with a beginner.

Type the accompanying code in any content manager or an IDE and spare it as helloWor

Variables

Step by step instructions to Declare and utilize a Variable

Let see a model. We will pronounce variable "an" and print it.

a=100

print a

Re-pronounce a Variable

You can re-pronounce the variable significantly after you have proclaimed it once.

Here we have variable instated to f=0.

Afterward, we re-relegate the variable f to esteem "guru99"

Factors in Python

Python 2 Example

Declare a variable and introduce it

f = 0

print f

re-pronouncing the variable works

f = 'guru99'

print f

Python 3 Example

Declare a variable and introduce it

f = 0

print(f)

re-proclaiming the variable works

f = 'guru99'

print(f)

Link Variables

How about we see whether you can connect various information types like string and number together. For instance, we will connect "Master" with the number "99".

In contrast to Java, which connects number with string without announcing number as string, Python requires proclaiming the number as string else it will show a TypeError

Factors in Python

For the accompanying code, you will get vague yield -

a="Guru"

b = 99

print a+b

When the whole number is proclaimed as string, it can connect both "Master" + str("99")= "Guru99" in the yield.

a="Guru"

b = 99

print(a+str(b))

Neighborhood and Global Variables

In Python when you need to utilize a similar variable for rest of your program or module you announce it a worldwide variable, while on the off chance that you need to utilize the variable in a particular capacity or technique, you utilize a nearby factor.

We should comprehend this contrast among nearby and worldwide variable with the beneath program.

Variable "f" is worldwide in scope and is appointed worth 101 which is imprinted in yield

Variable f is again proclaimed in work and expect neighborhood scope. It is allocated esteem "I am learning Python." which is printed out as a yield. This variable is not quite the same as the worldwide variable "f" characterize prior

When the capacity bring is finished, the neighborhood variable f is pulverized. At line 12, when we once more, print the estimation of "f" is it shows the estimation of worldwide variable f=101

Factors in Python

Python 2 Example

```python
# Declare a variable and introduce it

f = 101

print f

# Global versus nearby factors in capacities

def someFunction():
# worldwide f

f = 'I am learning Python'

print f

someFunction()


print f
```

Python 3 Example

Declare a variable and introduce it

f = 101

print(f)

Global versus nearby factors in capacities

def someFunction():

worldwide f

f = 'I am learning Python'

print(f)

someFunction()

print(f)

Utilizing the catchphrase worldwide, you can reference the worldwide variable inside a capacity.

Variable "f" is worldwide in scope and is allocated esteem 101 which is imprinted in yield

Variable f is pronounced utilizing the catchphrase worldwide. This is definitely not a neighborhood variable, yet the equivalent worldwide variable announced before. Henceforth when we print its worth, the yield is 101

We changed the estimation of "f" inside the capacity. When the capacity bring is finished, the changed estimation of the variable "f" perseveres. At line 12, when we once more, print the estimation of "f" is it shows the worth "changing worldwide variable"

Factors in Python

Python 2 Example

```
f = 101;
print f
```


```
# Global vs.local factors in capacities
def someFunction():
worldwide f
print f
f = "changing worldwide variable"
someFunction()
print f
```

Python 3 Example

```
f = 101;
```

```
print(f)

# Global vs.local factors in capacities

def someFunction():

worldwide f

print(f)

f = "changing worldwide variable"

someFunction()

print(f)
```

Erase a variable

You can likewise erase variable utilizing the order del "variable name".

In the model underneath, we erased variable f, and when we continue to print it, we get mistake "variable name isn't characterized" which implies you have erased the variable.

Factors in Python

```
f = 11;



print(f)
```

del f

print(f)

Conventions when naming Python

Python Naming Conventions

1. General

Abstain from utilizing names that are excessively broad or excessively tedious. Find some kind of harmony between the two.

Terrible: data_structure, my_list, info_map, dictionary_for_the_purpose_of_storing_data_representing_word_definitions

Great: user_profile, menu_options, word_definitions

Try not to be an ass and name things "O", "l", or "I"

When utilizing CamelCase names, underwrite all letters of a shortening (for example HTTPServer)

2. Bundles

Bundle names ought to be all lower case

At the point when various words are required, an underscore should isolate them

It is normally desirable over stick to 1 word names

3. Modules

Module names ought to be all lower case

At the point when numerous words are required, an underscore should isolate them

It is generally desirable over stick to 1 word names

4. Classes

Class names ought to pursue the UpperCaseCamelCase show

Python's worked in classes, anyway are commonly lowercase words

Special case classes should end in "Mistake"

5. Worldwide (module-level) Variables

Worldwide factors ought to be all lowercase

Words in a worldwide variable name ought to be isolated by an underscore

6. Occasion Variables

Occasion variable names ought to be all lower case

Words in an occurrence variable name ought to be isolated by an underscore

Non-open example factors should start with a solitary underscore

In the event that a case name should be ravaged, two underscores may start its name

7. Strategies

Strategy names ought to be all lower case

Words in a technique name ought to be isolated by an underscore

Non-open strategy should start with a solitary underscore

In the event that a strategy name should be ruined, two underscores may start its name

8. Strategy Arguments

Occurrence techniques ought to have their first contention named 'self'.

Class strategies ought to have their first contention named 'cls'

9. Capacities

Capacity names ought to be all lower case

Words in a capacity name ought to be isolated by an underscore

10. Constants

Steady names must be completely promoted

Words in a consistent name ought to be isolated by an underscore

Chapter 2

Types of Variables

Factors are only saved memory areas to store esteems. This implies when you make a variable you save some space in memory.

In view of the information kind of a variable, the translator designates memory and chooses what can be put away in the held memory. In this way, by allotting various information types to factors, you can store whole numbers, decimals or characters in these factors.

Allocating Values to Variables

Python factors don't require express revelation to hold memory space. The assertion happens consequently when you allocate an incentive to a variable. The equivalent sign (=) is utilized to appoint esteems to factors.

The operand to one side of the = administrator is the name of the variable and the operand to one side of the = administrator is the worth put away in the variable. For instance −

#!/usr/canister/python

counter = 100 # A whole number task

miles = 1000.0 # A drifting point

name = "John" # A string

print counter

print miles

print name

Here, 100, 1000.0 and "John" are the qualities allocated to counter, miles, and name factors, separately. This creates the accompanying outcome −

100

1000.0

John

Numerous Assignment

Python enables you to dole out a solitary incentive to a few factors all the while. For instance −

a = b = c = 1

Here, a number item is made with the worth 1, and each of the three factors are appointed to a similar memory area. You can likewise dole out numerous items to different factors. For instance −

a,b,c = 1,2,"john"

Here, two whole number articles with values 1 and 2 are alloted to factors an and b separately, and one string object with the worth "john" is relegated to the variable c.

Standard Data Types

The information put away in memory can be of numerous sorts. For instance, an individual's age is put away as a numeric worth and their location is put away as alphanumeric characters. Python has different standard information types that are utilized to characterize the tasks conceivable on them and the capacity strategy for every one of them.

Python has five standard information types −

Numbers

String

Rundown

Tuple

Lexicon

Python Numbers

Number information types store numeric qualities. Number items are made when you allot an incentive to them. For instance −

var1 = 1

var2 = 10

You can likewise erase the reference to a number article by utilizing the del articulation. The grammar of the del explanation is −

del var1[,var2[,var3[...,varN]]]]

You can erase a solitary item or various articles by utilizing the del articulation. For instance −

del var

del var_a, var_b

Python bolsters four diverse numerical sorts −

int (marked numbers)

(long numbers, they can likewise be spoken to in octal and hexadecimal)

glide (coasting point genuine qualities)

(complex numbers)

Models

Here are a few instances of numbers −

int	long	float	complex
10	51924361L	0.0	3.14j
100	-0x19323L	15.20	45.j

- 786	0122L	-21.9	9.322e-36j	
080	0xDEFABCECBDAECBFBAEl		32.3+e18	
	.876j			
- 0490	535633629843L	-90.	-.6545+0J	
- 0x260	-052318172735L	-32.54e100	3e+26J	
0x69	-4721885298529L	70.2-E12	4.53e-7j	

Python enables you to utilize a lowercase l with long, however it is prescribed that you utilize just a capitalized L to evade perplexity with the number 1. Python shows long whole numbers with a capitalized L.

A mind boggling number comprises of an arranged pair of genuine skimming point numbers meant by x + yj, where x and y are the genuine numbers and j is the nonexistent unit.

Python Strings

Strings in Python are recognized as a bordering set of characters spoke to in the quotes. Python takes into consideration either matches of single or twofold statements. Subsets of strings can be taken utilizing the cut administrator ([ ] and [:]) with files beginning at 0 in the start of the string and working their way from - 1 toward the end.

The in addition to (+) sign is the string connection administrator and the reference mark (*) is the reiteration administrator. For instance −

```
#!/usr/canister/python

str = 'Hi World!'

print str # Prints total string
print str[0] # Prints first character of the string
print str[2:5] # Prints characters beginning from third to fifth
print str[2:] # Prints string beginning from third character
print str * 2 # Prints string multiple times
print str + "TEST" # Prints linked string
```

This will deliver the accompanying outcome −

Hi World!

H

llo

llo World!

Hi World!Hello World!

Hi World!TEST

Python Lists

Records are the most flexible of Python's compound information types. A rundown contains things isolated by commas and encased inside square sections ([]). Somewhat, records are like exhibits in C. One distinction between them is that every one of the things having a place with a rundown can be of various information type.

The qualities put away in a rundown can be gotten to utilizing the cut administrator ([ ] and [:]) with lists beginning at 0 in the start of the rundown and working their approach to end - 1. The in addition to (+) sign is the rundown connection administrator, and the indicator (*) is the redundancy administrator. For instance −

#!/usr/canister/python

list = ['abcd', 786 , 2.23, 'john', 70.2]

tinylist = [123, 'john']

print list # Prints total rundown

print list[0] # Prints first component of the rundown

print list[1:3] # Prints components beginning from second till third

print list[2:] # Prints components beginning from third component

print tinylist * 2 # Prints list multiple times

print list + tinylist # Prints connected records

This produce the accompanying outcome −

['abcd', 786, 2.23, 'john', 70.2]

abcd

[786, 2.23]

[2.23, 'john', 70.2]

[123, 'john', 123, 'john']

['abcd', 786, 2.23, 'john', 70.2, 123, 'john']

Python Tuples

A tuple is another succession information type that is like the rundown. A tuple comprises of various qualities isolated by commas. In contrast to records, notwithstanding, tuples are encased inside brackets.

Numbers

Python Numbers, Type Conversion and Mathematics

Number Data Type in Python

Python bolsters whole numbers, drifting point numbers and complex numbers. They are characterized as int, buoy and complex class in Python.

Numbers and skimming focuses are isolated by the nearness or nonattendance of a decimal point. 5 is whole number though 5.0 is a skimming point number.

Complex numbers are written in the structure, x + yj, where x is the genuine part and y is the fanciful part.

We can utilize the sort() capacity to realize which class a variable or a worth has a place with and isinstance() capacity to check on the off chance that it has a place with a specific class.

script.py

IPython Shell

Run

Controlled by DataCamp

While whole numbers can be of any length, a drifting point number is precise just up to 15 decimal places (the sixteenth spot is off base).

Numbers we manage ordinary are decimal (base 10) number framework. Be that as it may, software engineers (for the most part inserted developer) need to work with parallel (base 2), hexadecimal (base 16) and octal (base 8) number frameworks.

In Python, we can speak to these numbers by fittingly putting a prefix before that number. Following table records these prefix.

Number framework prefix for Python numbers

Number System	Prefix
Binary	'0b' or '0B'
Octal	'0o' or '0O'
Hexadecimal	'0x' or '0X'

Here are a few models

script.py

IPython Shell

Run

Controlled by DataCamp

At the point when you run the program, the yield will be:

107

253

13

Type Conversion

We can change over one sort of number into another. This is otherwise called intimidation.

Tasks like expansion, subtraction constrain whole number to glide certainly (naturally), in the event that one of the operand is drift.

>>> 1 + 2.0

3.0

We can see over that 1 (whole number) is constrained into 1.0 (drift) for expansion and the outcome is likewise a coasting point number.

We can likewise utilize worked in capacities like int(), buoy() and complex() to change over between types expressly. These capacity can even change over from strings.

>>> int(2.3)

2

>>> int(- 2.8)

- 2

>>> float(5)

5.0

>>> complex('3+5j')

(3+5j)

While changing over from buoy to whole number, the number gets shortened (whole number that is more like zero).

Python Decimal

Python worked in class skim plays out certain counts that may astound us. We as a whole realize that the total of 1.1 and 2.2 is 3.3, however Python appears to oppose this idea.

```
>>> (1.1 + 2.2) == 3.3
```

Bogus

What is happening?

For reasons unknown, drifting point numbers are executed in PC equipment as double portions, as PC just gets parallel (0 and 1). Because of this explanation, the majority of the decimal parts we know, can't be precisely put away in our PC.

How about we take a model. We can't speak to the portion 1/3 as a decimal number. This will give 0.33333333... which is boundlessly long, and we can just inexact it.

Transforms out decimal part 0.1 will result into an unendingly long paired portion of 0.000110011001100110011... what's more, our PC just stores a limited number of it.

This will just surmised 0.1 however never be equivalent. Thus, it is the impediment of our PC equipment and not a blunder in Python.

```
>>> 1.1 + 2.2
```

3.3000000000000003

To defeat this issue, we can utilize decimal module that accompanies Python. While gliding point numbers have accuracy up to 15 decimal places, the decimal module has client settable exactness.

script.py

IPython Shell

Run

Controlled by DataCamp

This module is utilized when we need to do decimal estimations like we learned in school.

It additionally protects centrality. We realize 25.50 kg is more precise than 25.5 kg as it has two critical decimal spots contrasted with one.

script.py

IPython Shell

Run

Fueled by DataCamp

Notice the trailing zeroes in the above model.

We may ask, why not actualize Decimal without fail, rather than skim? The primary explanation is effectiveness. Gliding call attention to are done should quicker than Decimal tasks.

When to utilize Decimal rather than skim?

We for the most part utilize Decimal in the accompanying cases.

At the point when we are making money related applications that need precise decimal portrayal.

At the point when we need to control the degree of accuracy required.

At the point when we need to execute the thought of critical decimal spots.

At the point when we need the tasks to be done as we did at school

Python Fractions

Python gives tasks including partial numbers through its portions module.

A portion has a numerator and a denominator, the two of which are numbers. This module has support for discerning number-crunching.

We can make Fraction protests in different manners.

script.py

IPython Shell

Run

Controlled by DataCamp

While making Fraction from glide, we may get some unordinary results. This is because of the defective twofold skimming point number portrayal as talked about in the past segment.

Luckily, Fraction enables us to launch with string also. This is the favored choices when utilizing decimal numbers.

script.py

IPython Shell

Run

Fueled by DataCamp

This datatype underpins every essential activity. Here are scarcely any models.

script.py

IPython Shell

Run

Fueled by DataCamp

Python Mathematics

Python offers modules like math and arbitrary to complete diverse arithmetic like trigonometry, logarithms, likelihood and insights, and so forth.

script.py

IPython Shell

Run

Fueled by DataCamp

Here is the full rundown capacities and characteristics accessible in Python math module.

script.py

Strings

Python Strings

String Literals

String literals in python are encompassed by either single quotes, or twofold quotes.

'hi' is equivalent to "hi".

You can show a string strict with the print() work:

Model

```
print("Hello")
```

```
print('Hello')
```

Dole out String to a Variable

Doling out a string to a variable is finished with the variable name pursued by an equivalent sign and the string:

Model

```
a = "Hi"
```

```
print(a)
```

Multiline Strings

You can dole out a multiline string to a variable by utilizing three statements:

Model

You can utilize three twofold statements:

a = """Lorem ipsum dolor sit amet,

consectetur adipiscing elit,

sed do eiusmod tempor incididunt

ut labore et dolore magna aliqua."""

print(a)

Or on the other hand three single statements:

Model

a = '''Lorem ipsum dolor sit amet,

consectetur adipiscing elit,

sed do eiusmod tempor incididunt

ut labore et dolore magna aliqua.'''

print(a)

Note: in the outcome, the line breaks are embedded at a similar situation as in the code.

Strings are Arrays

In the same way as other famous programming dialects, strings in Python are varieties of bytes speaking to unicode characters.

In any case, Python doesn't have a character information type, a solitary character is essentially a string with a length of 1.

Square sections can be utilized to get to components of the string.

Model

Get the character at position 1 (recollect that the main character has the position 0):

a = "Hi, World!"

print(a[1])

Cutting

You can restore a scope of characters by utilizing the cut linguistic structure.

Determine the beginning list and the end list, isolated by a colon, to restore a piece of the string.

Model

Get the characters from position 2 to situate 5 (excluded):

b = "Hi, World!"

print(b[2:5])

Negative Indexing

Utilize negative files to begin the cut from the finish of the string:

Model

Get the characters from position 5 to situate 1, beginning the check from the finish of the string:

b = "Hi, World!"

print(b[-5:- 2])

String Length

To get the length of a string, utilize the len() work.

Model

The len() work restores the length of a string:

a = "Hi, World!"

print(len(a))

String Methods

Python has a lot of implicit techniques that you can use on strings.

Model

The strip() technique expels any whitespace from the earliest starting point or the end:

a = " Hello, World! "

print(a.strip()) # returns "Hi, World!"

Model

The lower() technique restores the string in lower case:

a = "Hi, World!"

print(a.lower())

Model

The upper() technique restores the string in capitalized:

a = "Hi, World!"

print(a.upper())

Model

The supplant() strategy replaces a string with another string:

a = "Hi, World!"

print(a.replace("H", "J"))

Model

The split() strategy parts the string into substrings on the off chance that it discovers occurrences of the separator:

a = "Hi, World!"

print(a.split(",")) # returns ['Hello', ' World!']

Become familiar with String Methods with our String Methods Reference

Check String

To check if a specific expression or character is available in a string, we can utilize the catchphrases in or not in.

Model

Check if the expression "ain" is available in the accompanying content:

```
txt = "The downpour in Spain stays chiefly in the plain"

x = "ain" in txt

print(x)
```

Model

Check if the expression "ain" is absent in the accompanying content:

```
txt = "The downpour in Spain stays fundamentally in the plain"

x = "ain" not in txt

print(x)
```

String Concatenation

To connect, or join, two strings you can utilize the + administrator.

Model

Union variable a with variable b into variable c:

```
a = "Hi"
```

b = "World"

c = a + b

print(c)

Keywords and Identifiers in Pythong Programming Language

Python Keywords and Identifiers

In this instructional exercise, you will find out about watchwords (saved words in Python) and identifiers (names given to factors, capacities, and so on.).

Python Keywords

Watchwords are the saved words in Python.

We can't utilize a watchword as a variable name, work name or some other identifier. They are utilized to characterize the punctuation and structure of the Python language.

In Python, watchwords are case delicate.

There are 33 watchwords in Python 3.7. This number can change marginally over the span of time.

Every one of the watchwords aside from True, False and None are in lowercase and they should be composed all things considered. The rundown of the considerable number of catchphrases is given beneath.

Watchwords in Python

False	class	finally	is	return
None	continue	for	lambda	try
True	def	from	nonlocal	while
and	del	global	not	with

as		elif	if	or	yield

assert		else	import pass

break		except	in	raise

Taking a gander at all the watchwords without a moment's delay and attempting to make sense of what they mean may be overpowering.

In the event that you need to have a diagram, here is the finished rundown of the considerable number of catchphrases with models.

Python Identifiers

An identifier is a name given to elements like class, capacities, factors, and so forth. It separates one element from another.

Rules for composing identifiers

Identifiers can be a mix of letters in lowercase (start to finish) or capitalized (a to z) or digits (0 to 9) or an underscore _. Names like myClass, var_1 and print_this_to_screen, all are substantial model.

An identifier can't begin with a digit. 1variable is invalid, yet variable1 is flawlessly fine.

Watchwords can't be utilized as identifiers.

>>> worldwide = 1

Record "<interactive input>", line 1

worldwide = 1

^

SyntaxError: invalid language structure

We can't utilize extraordinary images like !, @, #, $, % and so forth in our identifier.

```
>>> a@ = 0
```

Record "<interactive input>", line 1

a@ = 0

^

SyntaxError: invalid language structure

Identifier can be of any length.

Comments and Statements

Python Statement, Indentation and Comments

In this article, you will find out about Python proclamations, why space is significant and utilization of remarks in programming.

Python Statement

Directions that a Python translator can execute are called articulations. For instance, a = 1 is a task explanation. on the off chance that announcement, for articulation, while proclamation and so on are different sorts of explanations which will be talked about later.

Multi-line proclamation

In Python, end of an announcement is set apart by a newline character. Be that as it may, we can create an impression stretch out over different lines with the line continuation character (\). For instance:

```
a = 1 + 2 + 3 + \
```

```
4 + 5 + 6 + \
```

```
7 + 8 + 9
```

This is unequivocal line continuation. In Python, line continuation is inferred inside enclosures ( ), sections [ ] and supports { }. For example, we can actualize the above multi-line proclamation as

```
a = (1 + 2 + 3 +
```

```
4 + 5 + 6 +
```

```
7 + 8 + 9)
```

Here, the encompassing enclosures ( ) do the line continuation certainly. Same is the situation with [ ] and { }. For instance:

```python
hues = ['red',

'blue',

'green']
```

We could likewise place numerous announcements in a solitary line utilizing semicolons, as pursues

```python
a = 1; b = 2; c = 3
```

Python Indentation

The greater part of the programming dialects like C, C++, Java use props { } to characterize a square of code. Python utilizes space.

A code square (body of a capacity, circle and so on.) begins with space and finishes with the first unindented line. The measure of space is up to you, however it must be steady all through that square.

For the most part four whitespaces are utilized for space and is favored over tabs. Here is a model.

script.py

IPython Shell

Run

The requirement of space in Python makes the code look slick and clean. This outcomes into Python programs that appear to be comparative and reliable.

Space can be overlooked in line continuation. Yet, it's a smart thought to consistently indent. It makes the code increasingly lucid. For instance:

assuming True:

print('Hello')

a = 5

also,

assuming True: print('Hello'); a = 5

both are legitimate and do something very similar. Be that as it may, the previous style is more clear.

Mistaken space will result into IndentationError.

Python Comments

Remarks are significant while composing a program. It portrays what's happening inside a program so an individual taking a gander at the source code doesn't make some hard memories making sense of it. You may overlook the key subtleties of the program you just wrote in a month's time. So setting aside effort to clarify these ideas in type of remarks is constantly productive.

In Python, we utilize the hash (#) image to begin composing a remark.

It stretches out up to the newline character. Remarks are for software engineers for better comprehension of a program. Python Interpreter disregards remark.

#This is a remark

#print out Hello

print('Hello')

Multi-line remarks

On the off chance that we have remarks that expand various lines, one method for doing it is to utilize hash (#) in the start of each line. For instance:

#This is a long remark

#and it expands

#to numerous lines

Another method for doing this is to utilize triple statements, either '" or """.

These triple statements are commonly utilized for multi-line strings. However, they can be utilized as multi-line remark also. Except if they are not docstrings, they don't produce any additional code.

"""This is additionally a

ideal case of

multi-line remarks"""

Docstring in Python

Docstring is short for documentation string.

It is a string that happens as the main articulation in a module, capacity, class, or strategy definition. We should compose what a capacity/class does in the docstring.

Triple statements are utilized while composing docstrings. For instance:

script.py

IPython Shell

Run

Controlled by DataCamp

Docstring is accessible to us as the quality_doc__ of the capacity. Issue the accompanying code in shell once you run the above program.

Identation in Python

Proclamation, Indentation and Comment in Python

Proclamations

Guidelines written in the source code for execution are called articulations. There are various sorts of articulations in the Python programming language like Assignment explanation, Conditional proclamation, Looping articulations and so forth. These all assistance the client to get the necessary yield. For instance, n = 50 is a task explanation.

Multi-Line Statements: Statements in Python can be reached out to at least one lines utilizing enclosures (), props {}, square sections [], semi-colon (;), continuation character cut (\). At the point when the software engineer needs to do long computations and can't accommodate his announcements into one line, one can utilize these characters.

Model :

Proclaimed utilizing Continuation Character (\):

```
s = 1 + 2 + 3 + \

4 + 5 + 6 + \

7 + 8 + 9
```

Proclaimed utilizing brackets () :

n = (1 * 2 * 3 + 7 + 8 + 9)

Proclaimed utilizing square sections [] :

footballer = ['MESSI',

'NEYMAR',

'SUAREZ']

Proclaimed utilizing supports {} :

x = {1 + 2 + 3 + 4 + 5 + 6 +

7 + 8 + 9}

Proclaimed utilizing semicolons(;) :

banner = 2; ropes = 3; post = 4

Space

A square is a blend of every one of these announcements. Square can be viewed as the gathering of proclamations for a particular reason. The vast majority of the programming dialects like C, C++, Java use props { } to characterize a square of code. One of the particular highlights of Python is its utilization of space to feature the squares of code. Whitespace is utilized for space in Python. All announcements with a similar separation to the privilege have a place with a similar square of code. On the off chance that a square must be all the more profoundly settled, it is just indented further to one side. You can comprehend it better by taking a gander at the accompanying lines of code:

filter_none

alter

play_arrow

brightness_4

Python program appearing

space

site = 'gfg'

in the event that site == 'gfg':

print('Logging on to geeksforgeeks...')

else:

```python
print('retype the URL.')
```

```python
print('All set !')
```

Yield:

```
Signing on to geeksforgeeks...
```

```
All set !
```

The lines print('Logging on to geeksforgeeks... ') and print('retype the URL.') are two separate code squares. The two squares of code in our model if-explanation are both indented four spaces. The last print('All set!') isn't indented, thus it doesn't have a place with the else-square.

filter_none

alter

play_arrow

brightness_4

```
j = 1

while(j <= 5):

    print(j)

    j = j + 1
```

Yield:

1

2

3

4

5

To demonstrate a square of code in Python, you should indent each line of the square by the equivalent whitespace. The two lines of code in the while circle are both indented four spaces. It is required for showing what square of code an announcement has a place with. For instance, j=1 and while(j<=5): isn't indented, thus it isn't inside while square. Along these lines, Python code structures by space.

Remarks

Python designers frequently utilize the remark framework as, without its utilization, things can get genuine befuddling, genuine quick. Remarks are the valuable data that the designers give to cause the peruser to comprehend the source code. It clarifies the rationale or a piece of it utilized in the code. Remarks are normally useful to somebody keeping up or upgrading your code when you are never again around to address inquiries regarding it. These are regularly refered to as a valuable programming show that doesn't participate in the yield of the program yet improves the coherence of the entire program. There are two kinds of remark in Python:

Single line remarks : Python single line remark begins with hashtag image with no blank areas (#) and endures till the stopping point. In the event that the remark surpasses one line, at that point put a hashtag on the following line and proceed with the remark. Python's single line remarks are demonstrated valuable for providing short clarifications for factors, work revelations, and articulations. See the accompanying code scrap exhibiting single line remark:

Code 1:

filter_none

alter

play_arrow

brightness_4

This is a remark

Print "GeeksforGeeks !" to reassure

print("GeeksforGeeks")

Code 2:

filter_none

alter

play_arrow

brightness_4

a, b = 1, 3 # Declaring two numbers

entirety = a + b # including two whole numbers

print(sum) # showing the yield

Multi-line string as remark : Python multi-line remark is a bit of content encased in a delimiter (""") on each finish of the remark. Again there ought to be no void area between delimiter ("""). They are helpful when the remark content doesn't fit into one line; in this way needs to range crosswise over lines. Multi-line remarks or passages fill in as documentation for others perusing your code. See the accompanying code bit exhibiting multi-line remark:

Code 1:

filter_none

alter

play_arrow

brightness_4

"""

This would be a multiline remark in Python that

ranges a few lines and portrays geeksforgeeks.

A Computer Science entryway for nerds. It contains

elegantly composed, all around thought

what's more, well-clarified software engineering

tests and that's only the tip of the iceberg.

…

"""

print("GeeksForGeeks")

Code 2:

filter_none

alter

play_arrow

brightness_4

ideal case of

multi-line remarks'"

print("GeeksForGeeks")

Multiline Comments

Step by step instructions to Write Comment and Multiline

Remarks resemble signs which make a given code plainly obvious and profoundly comprehensible. In Python, we can include single-line and multi-line Python remark. This instructional exercise will cover both these techniques in detail. In the wake of understanding this, you would realize how to include a Python remark and which style to utilize.

Composing remarks is a decent programming practice. They are non-executable piece of the code, yet very basic in a program. These not just help different software engineers chipping away at a similar task however the analyzers can likewise allude them for lucidity on white-box testing.

It is ideal to include remarks while you make or update a program else you may lose the specific circumstance. What's more, remarks composed later may not be as viable as they ought to be.

+ Read: Statement, Expression and Indentation in Python

How To Use Comments In Python?

How to utilize single line remark in Python?

How to utilize multiline remarks in Python?

Utilizing hash mark for remarking

How to utilize docstrings in Python?

Utilizing triple-quote for docstring

docstring versus remark in Python

Python Comment, Multiline Comment, and DocString

Remarking is a specialty of communicating what a program will do at an exceptionally significant level. These are labeled lines of content to clarify a bit of code. In Python, we can apply two styles of remark: single-line and multiline.

Single-Line Python Comment

You may want to utilize a solitary line Python remark when there is need of short, snappy remarks for troubleshooting. Single-line remarks start with a pound (#) image and naturally finishes with an EOL (stopping point).

```python
# Good code is self-recording.

print("Learn Python Step by Step!")
```

While putting a remark, ensure your remark is at a similar indent level as the code underneath it. For instance, you may comment on a capacity definition which doesn't have any space. In any case, the capacity could have squares of code indented at various levels. So deal with the arrangement, when you remark inside the inner code squares.

Define a rundown of months

months = ['Jan', 'Feb', 'Blemish', 'Apr', 'May', 'Jun', 'Jul','Aug','Sep','Oct','Nov','Dec']

Function to print the calender months

def showCalender(months):

For circle that crosses the rundown and prints the name of every month

for month in months:

print(month)

showCalender(months)

Back to top

Multiline Python Comment

Python enables remarks to length over various lines. Such remarks are known as multiline or square remarks. You can utilize this style of remarking to depict something increasingly entangled.

This all-encompassing type of remarks applies to a few or the entirety of the code that pursues. Here is a guide to utilize the multiline Python remark.

Utilizing The Hash (#) Mark

To include multiline remarks, you should start each fix with the pound (#) image pursued by a solitary space. You can isolate a remark into passages. Simply include a vacant line with a hash mark between every para.

Note: The image (#) is otherwise called the octothorpe. The term originated from a gathering of designers at Bell Labs while dealing with a first of the touch-tone keypads venture.

To Learn any language you should keep the beneath rules.

1. Know the fundamental sentence structure, information types, control structures and contingent proclamations.

2. Learn mistake taking care of and document I/O.

3. Find out about cutting edge information structures.

4. Compose works and pursue OOPs ideas.

def primary():

print("Let's begin to learn Python.")

...

Docstring In Python

Python has the documentation strings (or docstrings) highlight. It gives software engineers a simple method for including snappy notes with each Python module, capacity, class, and technique.

You can characterize a docstring by including it as a string consistent. It must be the primary proclamation in the article's (module, capacity, class, and technique) definition.

The docstring has an a lot more extensive degree than a Python remark. Consequently, it ought to portray what the capacity does, not how. Likewise, it is a decent practice for all elements of a program to have a docstring.

How To Define Docstring In Python?

You can characterize a docstring with the assistance of triple-quote. Include one in the first place and second toward the finish of the string. Much the same as multiline remarks, docstring can likewise cover to various lines.

Note: The strings characterized utilizing triple-quote are docstring in Python. Be that as it may, it may appear to you as a normal remark.

What Is The Difference Between A Comment And The Docstring?

The strings starting with triple statements are as yet ordinary strings aside from the way that they could spread to various lines. It implies they are executable proclamations. What's more, in the event that they are not marked, at that point they will be trash gathered when the code executes.

The Python translator won't disregard them as it does with the remarks. Be that as it may, if such a string is put following a capacity or class definition or over a module, at that point they transform into docstrings. You can get to them utilizing the accompanying extraordinary variable.

myobj.__doc__

Model

```python
def theFunction():

    '''

    This capacity show the utilization of docstring in Python.


    '''


print("Python docstrings are not remarks.")

print("\nJust printing the docstring value...")

print(theFunction._doc__)
```

Wrap Up – Python Comment And Docstring

Remarks and docstrings add esteems to a program. They make your projects increasingly discernible and viable. Regardless of whether you have to refactor a similar code later, at that point it is simpler to do with remarks accessible.

Programming invests just 10% energy of its life being developed and rest of 90% in upkeep.

Henceforth, consistently put pertinent and helpful remarks or docstrings as they lead to more coordinated effort and accelerate the code refactoring exercises.

Phyton's Docstring

It's predefined in source code that is utilized, similar to a remark, to record a particular fragment of code. Dissimilar to traditional source code remarks, the docstring ought to portray what the capacity does, not how.

What should a docstring resemble?

The doc string line should start with a capital letter and end with a period.

The main line ought to be a short portrayal.

On the off chance that there are more lines in the documentation string, the subsequent line ought to be clear, outwardly isolating the outline from the remainder of the depiction.

The accompanying lines ought to be at least one passages depicting the item's calling shows, its reactions, and so forth.

Announcing Docstrings: The docstrings are proclaimed utilizing """triple twofold statements""" just beneath the class, technique or capacity affirmation. All capacities ought to have a docstring.

Getting to Docstrings: The docstrings can be gotten to utilizing the __doc__ technique for the item or utilizing the assistance work.

The beneath model exhibits how to announce and get to a docstring.

filter_none

alter

play_arrow

brightness_4

```
def my_function():

"""Exhibit docstrings and does nothing really."""

return None

print "Utilizing_doc_:"

print my_function.__doc__

print "Utilizing help:"

help(my_function)
```

Yield:

Utilizing _doc_:

Exhibit docstrings and does nothing truly.

Utilizing help:

Help on work my_function in module _main_:

my_function()

Exhibit docstrings and does nothing truly.

One-line Docstrings

As the name proposes, one line docstrings fit in one line. They are utilized in evident cases. The end cites are on a similar line as the opening statements. This searches better for jokes.

For instance:

filter_none

alter

play_arrow

brightness_4

def power(a, b):

"""Returns arg1 raised to control arg2."""

return a**b

print power.__doc__

Yield:

Returns arg1 raised to control arg2.

Multi-line Docstrings

Multi-line docstrings comprise of a synopsis line simply like a one-line docstring, trailed by a clear line, trailed by a progressively intricate depiction. The rundown line might be on a similar line as the opening statements or on the following line.

The model underneath shows a multi-line docstring.

filter_none

alter

play_arrow

brightness_4

def my_function(arg1):

"""

Outline line.

Expanded portrayal of capacity.

Parameters:

arg1 (int): Description of arg1

Returns:

int: Description of return esteem

"""

return arg1

print my_function.__doc__

Yield:

Synopsis line.

Expanded portrayal of capacity.

Parameters:

arg1 (int): Description of arg1

Returns:

int: Description of return esteem

Space in Docstrings

The whole docstring is indented equivalent to the statements at its first line. Docstring handling instruments will strip a uniform measure of space from the second and further lines of the docstring, equivalent to the base space of all non-clear lines after the principal line. Any space in the principal line of the docstring (i.e., up to the first newline) is inconsequential and evacuated. Relative space of later lines in the docstring is held.

Docstrings in Classes

Let us take a guide to tell the best way to compose docstrings for a class and its strategies. help is utilized to get to the docstring.

filter_none

alter

play_arrow

brightness_4

class ComplexNumber:

"""

This is a class for scientific tasks on complex numbers.

Properties:

genuine (int): The genuine piece of complex number.

imag (int): The fanciful piece of complex number.

"""

def_init_(self, genuine, imag):

"""

The constructor for ComplexNumber class.

Parameters:

genuine (int): The genuine piece of complex number.

imag (int): The nonexistent piece of complex number.

"""

def add(self, num):

"""

The capacity to include two Complex Numbers.

Parameters:

num (ComplexNumber): The intricate number to be included.

Returns:

ComplexNumber: An intricate number which contains the aggregate.

"""

re = self.real + num.real

im = self.imag + num.imag

return ComplexNumber(re, im)

help(ComplexNumber) # to get to Class docstring

help(ComplexNumber.add) # to get to strategy's docstring

Yield:

Help on class ComplexNumber in module_main_:

class ComplexNumber

| This is a class for numerical tasks on complex numbers.

|

| Attributes:

| genuine (int): The genuine piece of complex number.

| imag (int): The fanciful piece of complex number.

| Methods characterized here:

|_init_(self, genuine, imag)

| The constructor for ComplexNumber class.

| Parameters:

| genuine (int): The genuine piece of complex number.

| imag (int): The nonexistent piece of complex number.

| add(self, num)

| The capacity to include two Complex Numbers.

| Parameters:

| num (ComplexNumber): The perplexing number to be included.

| Returns:

| ComplexNumber: A perplexing number which contains the whole.

Help on technique include module_main_:

add(self, num) unbound_main_.ComplexNumber technique

The capacity to include two Complex Numbers.

Parameters:

num (ComplexNumber): The mind boggling number to be included.

Returns:

ComplexNumber: A mind boggling number which contains the aggregate.

This research is contributed by Mayank Agrawal. On the off chance that you like GeeksforGeeks and might want to contribute, you can likewise compose an article utilizing contribute.geeksforgeeks.org or mail your article to contribute@geeksforgeeks.org. See your article showing up on the GeeksforGeeks principle page and help different Geeks.

Operators in Python

Administrators are the builds which can control the estimation of operands.

Consider the articulation 4 + 5 = 9. Here, 4 and 5 are called operands and + is called administrator.

Kinds of Operator

Python language bolsters the accompanying sorts of administrators.

Number juggling Operators

Examination (Relational) Operators

Task Operators

Sensible Operators

Bitwise Operators

Participation Operators

Character Operators

Let us view all administrators individually.

Python Arithmetic Operators

Expect variable a holds 10 and variable b holds 20, at that point −

[Show Example]

Operator   Description   Example

+ Addition   Adds values on either side of the operator.
        a + b = 30

- Subtraction Subtracts right hand operand from left hand operand.   a − b = − 10

* Multiplication   Multiplies values on either side of the operator   a * b = 200

/Division   Divides left hand operand by right hand operand   b/a = 2

% Modulus   Divides left hand operand by right hand operand and returns remainder   b % a = 0

** Exponent Performs exponential (control) computation on operators   a**b =10 to the power 20

/   Floor Division - The division of operands where the outcome is the remainder wherein the digits after the decimal point are expelled. In any case, on the off chance that one of the operands is negative, the outcome is stunned, i.e., adjusted away from zero (towards negative limitlessness) –   9//2 = 4 and 9.0//2.0 = 4.0, - 11//3 = - 4, - 11.0//3 = - 4.0

Python Comparison Operators

These administrators think about the qualities on either sides of them and choose the connection among them. They are likewise called Relational administrators.

Expect variable a holds 10 and variable b holds 20, at that point −

Operator   Description   Example

==   If the estimations of two operands are equivalent, at that point the condition becomes true.   (a == b) isn't valid.

!=   If estimations of two operands are not approach, at that point condition becomes true.   (a != b) is valid.

<> If estimations of two operands are not approach, at that point condition becomes true. (a <> b) is valid. This is like != administrator.

>   If the estimation of left operand is more prominent than the estimation of right operand, at that point condition becomes true. (a > b) isn't valid.

<   If the estimation of left operand is not exactly the estimation of right operand, at that point condition becomes true.   (a < b) is valid.

>=   If the estimation of left operand is more prominent than or equivalent to the estimation of right operand, at that point condition becomes true.   (a >= b) isn't valid.

<= If the estimation of left operand is not exactly or equivalent to the estimation of right operand, at that point condition becomes true.   (a <= b) is valid.

Python Assignment Operators

Expect variable a holds 10 and variable b holds 20, at that point –

Operator   Description   Example

=   Assigns values from right side operands to left side operand   c = a + b allocates estimation of a + b into c

+= Add AND It adds right operand to one side operand and dole out the outcome to left operand c += an is comparable to c = c + a

- = Subtract AND   It subtracts right operand from the left operand and allot the outcome to left operand   c - = an is identical to c = c - a

*= Multiply AND   It duplicates right operand with the left operand and dole out the outcome to left operand
        c *= an is identical to c = c * a

/= Divide AND   It separates left operand with the correct operand and appoint the outcome to left operand   c/= an is proportional to c = c/a

%= Modulus AND   It takes modulus utilizing two operands and appoint the outcome to left operand   c %= an is equal to c = c % a

**= Exponent AND Performs exponential (control) count on administrators and appoint an incentive to one side operand   c **= an is equal to c = c ** a

/= Floor Division   It performs floor division on administrators and dole out an incentive to one side operand   c/= an is proportionate to c = c/a

Python Bitwise Operators

Bitwise administrator chips away at bits and performs a little bit at a time activity. Expect if a = 60; and b = 13; Now in the double arrangement their qualities will be 0011 1100 and 0000 1101 separately. Following table records out the bitwise administrators bolstered by Python language with a model each in those, we utilize the over two factors (an and b) as operands −

a = 0011 1100

b = 0000 1101

- -

a&b = 0000 1100

a|b = 0011 1101

a^b = 0011 0001

~a = 1100 0011

There are following Bitwise administrators bolstered by Python language

Operator   Description   Example

and Binary AND   Operator duplicates a piece to the outcome on the off chance that it exists in both operands   (a and b) (implies 0000 1100)

| Binary OR   It duplicates a piece in the event that it exists in either operand.   (a | b) = 61 (implies 0011 1101)

^ Binary XORIt duplicates the bit in the event that it is set in one operand however not both.   (a ^ b) = 49 (implies 0011 0001)

~ Binary Ones Complement It is unary and has the impact of 'flipping' bits. (~a) = - 61 (implies 1100 0011 in 2's supplement structure because of a marked twofold number.

<< Binary Left Shift The left operands esteem is moved left by the quantity of bits indicated by the privilege operand.   a << 2 = 240 (implies 1111 0000)

>> Binary Right ShiftThe left operands esteem is moved right by the quantity of bits indicated by the privilege operand.   a >> 2 = 15 (implies 0000 1111)

Python Logical Operators

There are following intelligent administrators bolstered by Python language. Expect variable a holds 10 and variable b holds 20 at that point

[Show Example]

Operator   Description   Example

what's more, Logical AND   If both the operands are genuine at that point condition becomes true.   (a and b) is valid.

or then again Logical OR If any of the two operands are non-zero at that point condition becomes true.   (a or b) is valid.

not Logical NOT Used to turn around the legitimate condition of its operand. Not(a and b) is bogus.

Python Membership Operators

Python's participation administrators test for enrollment in a succession, for example, strings, records, or tuples. There are two participation administrators as clarified beneath −

Operator   Description   Example

in   Evaluates to genuine on the off chance that it finds a variable in the predefined succession and bogus otherwise.
        x in y, here in brings about a 1 if x is an individual from grouping y.

not in   Evaluates to genuine on the off chance that it doesn't finds a variable in the predetermined succession and bogus otherwise.   x not in y, here not in brings about a 1 if x isn't an individual from grouping y.

Python Identity Operators

Personality administrators think about the memory areas of two items. There are two Identity administrators clarified beneath −

Operator   Description   Example

is   Evaluates to genuine if the factors on either side of the administrator point to a similar article and bogus otherwise.   x is y, here is brings about 1 if id(x) rises to id(y).

is not Evaluates to bogus if the factors on either side of the administrator point to a similar article and genuine otherwise.   x isn't y, here isn't brings about 1 if id(x) isn't equivalent to id(y).

Python Operators Precedence

The accompanying table records all administrators from most elevated priority to least.

Sr.No. Operator and Description

1

**

Exponentiation (raise to the power)

2

~ + -

Supplement, unary in addition to and less (technique names
for the last two are +@ and - @)

3

* / % /

Increase, partition, modulo and floor division

4

+ -

Expansion and subtraction

5

>> <<

Right and left bitwise move

6

and

Bitwise 'AND'

7

^ |

Bitwise restrictive 'OR' and normal 'OR'

8

<= <>>=

Correlation administrators

9

<> == !=

Fairness administrators

10

= %=/=/= - = += *= **=

Task administrators

11

is isn't

Personality administrators

12

in not in

Enrollment administrators

13

not or and

Coherent administrators

Chapter 3

Functions in Python

Capacities in Python

A capacity is a lot of articulations that take inputs, do some particular calculation and produces yield. The thought is to put some usually or over and again done assignment together and make a capacity, so that as opposed to composing a similar code over and over for various sources of info, we can call the capacity.

Python gives worked in capacities like print(), and so on however we can likewise make your very own capacities. These capacities are called client characterized capacities.

filter_none

alter

play_arrow

brightness_4

A basic Python capacity to check

whether x is even or odd

```python
def evenOdd( x ):
```

in the event that (x % 2 == 0):

print "even"

else:

print "odd"

Driver code

evenOdd(2)

evenOdd(3)

Yield:

indeed

odd

Pass by Reference or pass by esteem?

One significant thing to note is, in Python each factor name is a reference. At the point when we pass a variable to a capacity, another reference to the item is made. Parameter going in Python is same as reference going in Java.

filter_none

alter

play_arrow

brightness_4

Here x is another reference to same rundown lst

def myFun(x):

x[0] = 20

Driver Code (Note that lst is adjusted

after capacity call.

lst = [10, 11, 12, 13, 14, 15]

myFun(lst);

print(lst)

Yield:

[20, 11, 12, 13, 14, 15]

At the point when we pass a reference and change the got reference to something different, the association among passed and got parameter is broken. For instance, consider beneath program.

filter_none

alter

play_arrow

brightness_4

```
def myFun(x):

# After beneath line connection of x with past

# object gets broken. Another item is relegated

# to x.

x = [20, 30, 40]

# Driver Code (Note that lst isn't changed

# after capacity call.

lst = [10, 11, 12, 13, 14, 15]

myFun(lst);

print(lst)
```

Yield:

[10, 11, 12, 13, 14, 15]

Another guide to exhibit that reference connect is broken in the event that we allot another worth (inside the capacity).

filter_none

alter

play_arrow

brightness_4

```python
def myFun(x):

    # After beneath line connection of x with past

    # object gets broken. Another article is alloted

    # to x.

    x = 20

# Driver Code (Note that lst isn't changed

# after capacity call.

x = 10

myFun(x);

print(x)
```

Yield:

10

Exercise: Try to figure the yield of following code.

filter_none

alter

play_arrow

brightness_4

```python
def swap(x, y):

temp = x;

x = y;

y = temp;

# Driver code

x = 2

y = 3


swap(x, y)

print(x)

print(y)
```

Yield:

2

3

Default contentions:

A default contention is a parameter that accept a default esteem if a worth isn't given in the capacity call to that argument.The following model outlines Default contentions.

filter_none

alter

play_arrow

brightness_4

Python program to illustrate

default contentions

def myFun(x, y=50):

print("x: ", x)

print("y: ", y)

Driver code (We call myFun() with as it were

contention)

myFun(10)

Yield:

('x: ', 10)

('y: ', 50)

Like C++ default contentions, any number of contentions in a capacity can have a default esteem. In any case, when we have a default contention, every one of the contentions to its privilege should likewise have default esteems.

Watchword contentions:

The thought is to enable guest to indicate contention name with values so guest doesn't have to recollect request of parameters.

filter_none

alter

play_arrow

brightness_4

```python
# Python program to show Keyword Arguments
def student(firstname, lastname):
    print(firstname, lastname)

# Keyword contentions
```

student(firstname ='Geeks', lastname ='Practice')

student(lastname ='Practice', firstname ='Geeks')

Yield:

('Nerds', 'Practice')

('Nerds', 'Practice')

Variable length contentions:

We can have both ordinary and watchword variable number of contentions. If it's not too much trouble see this for subtleties.

filter_none

alter

play_arrow

brightness_4

Python program to outline

*args for variable number of contentions

def myFun(*argv):

for arg in argv:

```python
print (arg)

myFun('Hello', 'Welcome', 'to', 'GeeksforGeeks')
```

Yield:

```
Hi
Welcome
to
GeeksforGeeks
```

filter_none

alter

play_arrow

brightness_4

```python
# Python program to show
# *kargs for variable number of watchword contentions

def myFun(**kwargs):
    for key, esteem in kwargs.items():
        print ("%s == %s" %(key, esteem))

# Driver code
myFun(first ='Geeks', mid ='for', last='Geeks')
```

Chapter 4

Basic Functions in Python

Client Defined Functions in Python

Distributed Jul 19, 2016Last refreshed Jun 19, 2017

Client Defined Functions in Python

Capacities are normal to all programming dialects, and it very well may be characterized as a square of re-usable code to perform explicit errands. Be that as it may, characterizing capacities in Python implies knowing the two kinds first: implicit and client characterized. Worked in capacities are normally a piece of Python bundles and libraries, though client characterized capacities are composed by the designers to meet certain prerequisites. In Python, all capacities are treated as items, so it is increasingly adaptable contrasted with other elevated level dialects.

In this article, we will concentrate on the client characterized works in Python. To totally comprehend the idea, we will figure out how they can be executed by composing code models. How about we view other significant ideas before bouncing into coding.

Significance of client characterized works in Python

By and large, designers can compose client characterized capacities or it very well may be acquired as an outsider library. This additionally implies your very own client characterized capacities can likewise be an outsider library for different clients. Client characterized capacities have certain favorable circumstances depending when and how they are utilized. Let 's view the accompanying focuses.

Client characterized capacities are reusable code squares; they just should be composed once, at that point they can be utilized on numerous occasions. They can even be utilized in different applications, as well.

These capacities are exceptionally helpful, from composing normal utilities to explicit business rationale. These capacities can likewise be altered per necessity.

The code is generally efficient, simple to keep up, and designer benevolent. Which implies it can bolster the measured structure approach.

As client characterized capacities can be composed autonomously, the errands of a task can be circulated for fast application advancement.

A well-characterized and attentively composed client characterized capacity can facilitate the application advancement process.

Since we have a fundamental comprehension of the focal points, how about we view diverse capacity contentions in Python.

Capacity contentions in Python

In Python, client characterized capacities can take four
distinct kinds of contentions. The contention types and their
implications, notwithstanding, are pre-characterized and
can't be changed. In any case, an engineer can, rather, keep
these pre-characterized rules to make their very own
custom capacities. Coming up next are the four kinds of
contentions and their guidelines.

1. Default contentions:

Python has an alternate method for speaking to language
structure and default esteems for work contentions. Default
esteems show that the capacity contention will take that
worth if no contention esteem is passed during capacity
call. The default esteem is relegated by utilizing task (=)
administrator. The following is an average sentence
structure for default contention. Here, msg parameter has a
default esteem Hello!.

Capacity definition

```
def defaultArg( name, msg = "Hello!"):
```

Capacity call

```
defaultArg( name)
```

2. Required contentions:

Required contentions are the obligatory contentions of a capacity. These contention esteems must be passed in right number and request during capacity call. The following is a run of the mill sentence structure for a necessary contention work.

Capacity definition

```
def requiredArg (str,num):
```

Capacity call

```
requiredArg ("Hello",12)
```

3. Catchphrase contentions:

Catchphrase contentions are significant for Python work calls. The catchphrases are referenced during the capacity call alongside their comparing esteems. These watchwords are mapped with the capacity contentions so the capacity can without much of a stretch distinguish the relating esteems regardless of whether the request isn't kept up during the capacity call. Coming up next is the linguistic structure for watchword contentions.

Capacity definition

```
def keywordArg( name, job ):
```

Capacity call

keywordArg(name = "Tom", job = "Administrator")

or on the other hand

keywordArg(job = "Administrator", name = "Tom")

4. Variable number of contentions:

This is exceptionally helpful when we don't have the foggiest idea about the precise number of contentions that will be passed to a capacity. Or on the other hand we can have a structure where any number of contentions can be passed dependent on the prerequisite. The following is the language structure for this kind of capacity call.

Chapter 5

Data types in Python

Presently you realize how to connect with the Python mediator and execute Python code. It's a great opportunity to dive into the Python language. First up is an exchange of the fundamental information types that are incorporated with Python.

This is what you'll realize in this instructional exercise:

You'll find out around a few essential numeric, string, and Boolean sorts that are incorporated with Python. Before the finish of this instructional exercise, you'll be acquainted with what objects of these sorts resemble, and how to speak to them.

You'll likewise get a review of Python's worked in capacities. These are pre-composed lumps of code you can call to do valuable things. You have just observed the worked in print() work, however there are numerous others.

Take the Quiz: Test your insight with our intuitive "Fundamental Data Types in Python" test. Upon consummation you will get a score so you can follow your learning progress after some time:

Expel promotions

Whole numbers

In Python 3, there is adequately no restriction to what extent a whole number worth can be. Obviously, it is obliged by the measure of memory your framework has, just like all things, however past that a whole number can be the length of you need it to be:

>>>
print(123123123123123123123123123123123123123123123
23123 + 1)

123123123123123123123123123123123123123123123123124

Python translates a succession of decimal digits with no
prefix to be a decimal number:

>>> print(10)

10

The accompanying strings can be prepended to a whole
number an incentive to demonstrate a base other than 10:

Prefix Interpretation Base

0b (zero + lowercase letter 'b')

0B (zero + capitalized letter 'B')   Binary 2

0o (zero + lowercase letter 'o')

0O (zero + capitalized letter 'O')   Octal 8

0x (zero + lowercase letter 'x')

0X (zero + capitalized letter 'X')   Hexadecimal 16

For instance:

```
>>> print(0o10)
```

8

```
>>> print(0x10)
```

```
>>> print(0b10)
```

2

For more data on number qualities with non-decimal bases, see the accompanying Wikipedia destinations: Binary, Octal, and Hexadecimal.

The hidden kind of a Python whole number, independent of the base used to indicate it, is called int:

```
>>> type(10)
```

<class 'int'>

```
>>> type(0o10)
```

```
<class 'int'>
```

```
>>> type(0x10)
```

```
<class 'int'>
```

Note: This is a decent time to make reference to that on the off chance that you need to show a worth while in a REPL session, you don't have to utilize the print() work. Simply composing the incentive at the >>> brief and hitting Enter will show it:

```
>>> 10
```

```
10
```

```
>>> 0x10
```

16

```
>>> 0b10
```

2

A significant number of the models in this instructional exercise arrangement will utilize this element.

Note this doesn't work inside a content record. A worth showing up on a line without anyone else in a content record will do nothing.

Skimming Point Numbers

The buoy type in Python assigns a skimming point number. glide esteems are indicated with a decimal point. Alternatively, the character e or E pursued by a positive or negative whole number might be affixed to indicate logical documentation:

```
>>> 4.2
```

```
4.2
```

```
>>> type(4.2)
```

```
<class 'float'>
```

```
>>> 4.
```

```
4.0
```

```
>>> .2
```

```
0.2
```

```
>>> .4e7
```

```
4000000.0
```

```
>>> type(.4e7)
```

```
<class 'float'>
```

```
>>> 4.2e-4
```

```
0.00042
```

Profound Dive: Floating-Point Representation

Coming up next is more top to bottom data on how Python speaks to drifting point numbers inside. You can promptly utilize coasting point numbers in Python without understanding them to this level don't as well, stress if this appears to be excessively convoluted. The data is exhibited here in the event that you are interested.

Practically all stages speak to Python skim qualities as 64-piece "twofold exactness" values, as indicated by the IEEE 754 standard. All things considered, the most extreme worth a gliding point number can have is roughly 1.8 × 10308. Python will demonstrate a number more prominent than that by the string inf:

```
>>> 1.79e308
```

1.79e+308

```
>>> 1.8e308
```

inf

The nearest a nonzero number can be to zero is roughly 5.0 × 10-324. Anything closer to zero than that is successfully zero:

>>> 5e-324

5e-324

>>> 1e-325

0.0

Drifting point numbers are spoken to inside as twofold (base-2) portions. Most decimal divisions can't be spoken to precisely as paired parts, so as a rule the inner portrayal of a skimming point number is a guess of the real worth. By and by, the distinction between the genuine worth and the spoke to esteem is little and ought not as a rule cause noteworthy issues.

Further Reading: For extra data on coasting point portrayal in Python and the potential traps included, see Floating Point Arithmetic: Issues and Limitations in the Python documentation.

Complex Numbers

Complex numbers are indicated as <real part>+<imaginary part>j. For instance:

```
>>> 2+3j
```

```
(2+3j)
```

```
>>> type(2+3j)
```

```
<class 'complex'>
```

Strings

Strings are groupings of character information. The string type in Python is called str.

String literals might be delimited utilizing either single or twofold statements. Every one of the characters between the opening delimiter and coordinating shutting delimiter are a piece of the string:

```
>>> print("I am a string.")
```

I am a string.

```
>>> type("I am a string.")
```

```
<class 'str'>
```

```
>>> print('I am as well.')
```

I am as well.

```
>>> type('I am as well.')
```

```
<class 'str'>
```

A string in Python can contain the same number of characters as you wish. As far as possible is your machine's memory assets. A string can likewise be vacant:

```
>>> ''
```

```
''
```

Imagine a scenario in which you need to incorporate a statement character as a component of the string itself. Your first motivation may be to have a go at something like this:

```
>>> print('This string contains a solitary statement (')
character.')
```

```
SyntaxError: invalid language structure
```

As should be obvious, that doesn't work so well. The string
in this model opens with a solitary statement, so Python
expect the following single statement, the one in enclosures
which was proposed to be a piece of the string, is the end
delimiter. The last single statement is then a stray and
causes the sentence structure blunder appeared.

In the event that you need to incorporate either sort of
statement character inside the string, the least difficult route
is to delimit the string with the other kind. In the event that
a string is to contain a solitary statement, delimit it with
twofold statements and the other way around:

```
>>> print("This string contains a solitary statement (')
character.")
```

This string contains a solitary statement (') character.

>>> print('This string contains a twofold statement (") character.')

This string contains a twofold statement (") character.

Getaway Sequences in Strings

In some cases, you need Python to decipher a character or grouping of characters inside a string in an unexpected way. This may happen in one of two different ways:

You might need to stifle the unique translation that specific characters are typically given inside a string.

You might need to apply extraordinary understanding to characters in a string which would regularly be taken actually.

You can achieve this utilizing an oblique punctuation line (\) character. An oblique punctuation line character in a string shows that at least one characters that tail it ought to be dealt with uncommonly. (This is alluded to as a departure succession, in light of the fact that the oblique punctuation line causes the ensuing character arrangement to "get away from" its standard importance.)

We should perceive how this functions.

Stifling Special Character Meaning

You have just observed the issues you can face when you attempt to incorporate statement characters in a string. In the event that a string is delimited by single statements, you can't straightforwardly determine a solitary statement character as a component of the string on the grounds that, for that string, the single statement has uncommon importance—it ends the string:

```
>>> print('This string contains a solitary statement (')
character.')
```

SyntaxError: invalid sentence structure

Determining an oblique punctuation line before the statement character in a string "get away" it and makes Python smother its standard uncommon importance. It is then deciphered just as an exacting single statement character:

```
>>> print('This string contains a solitary statement (\')
character.')
```

This string contains a solitary statement (') character.

Similar works in a string delimited by twofold statements too:

```
>>> print("This string contains a twofold statement (\")
character.")
```

This string contains a twofold statement (") character.

Coming up next is a table of break successions which cause Python to smother the standard extraordinary translation of a character in a string:

Departure

Sequence   Usual Interpretation of

Character(s) After Backslash "Escaped" Interpretation

\'   Terminates string with single statement opening delimiter   Literal single statement (') character

\"		Terminates string with twofold statement opening

delimiter		Literal twofold statement (") character

\newline		Terminates input line Newline is disregarded

\\		Introduces escape sequence Literal oblique

punctuation line (\) character

Usually, a newline character ends line input. So squeezing

Enter in a string will make Python think it is fragmented:

>>> print('a

SyntaxError: EOL while checking string strict

To separate a string over more than one line, incorporate an

oblique punctuation line before each newline, and the

newlines will be overlooked:

>>> print('a\

... b\

... c')

abc

To incorporate an exacting oblique punctuation line in a string, escape it with an oblique punctuation line:

>>> print('foo\\bar')

foo\bar

Applying Special Meaning to Characters

Next, assume you have to make a string that contains a tab character in it. Some content tools may enable you to embed a tab character straightforwardly into your code. However, numerous developers think about that poor practice, for a few reasons:

The PC can recognize a tab character and a succession of room characters, however you can't. To a human perusing the code, tab and space characters are outwardly undefined.

Some content managers are arranged to naturally kill tab characters by growing them to the suitable number of spaces.

Some Python REPL conditions won't embed tabs into code.

In Python (and practically all other basic programming languages), a tab character can be determined by the getaway succession \t:

```
>>> print('foo\tbar')
```

foo bar

The break grouping \t causes the t character to lose its
standard importance, that of a strict t.

Chapter 6

Flow control in Python

4. More Control Flow Tools

Other than the while articulation just presented, Python utilizes the typical stream control explanations known from different dialects, with certain turns.

4.1. on the off chance that Statements

Maybe the most outstanding explanation type is the if proclamation. For instance:

```
>>>
```

```
>>> x = int(input("Please enter a whole number: "))
```

If you don't mind enter a whole number: 42

```python
>>> if x < 0:

... x = 0

... print('Negative changed to zero')

... elif x == 0:

... print('Zero')

... elif x == 1:

... print('Single')

... else:

... print('More')
```

...

More

There can be at least zero elif parts, and the else part is discretionary. The catchphrase 'elif' is short for 'else if', and is valuable to maintain a strategic distance from over the top space. An if ... elif ... elif ... arrangement subs for the switch or case articulations found in different dialects.

4.2. for Statements

The for explanation in Python varies a piece from what you might be utilized to in C or Pascal. As opposed to continually repeating over a math movement of numbers (like in Pascal), or enabling the client to characterize both the emphasis step and stopping condition (as C), Python's for articulation emphasizes over the things of any grouping (a rundown or a string), in the request that they show up in the succession. For instance (no joke expected):

```
>>>
```

```
>>> # Measure a few strings:
```

```
... words = ['cat', 'window', 'defenestrate']
```

```
>>> for w in words:
```

```
... print(w, len(w))
```

```
...
```

```
feline 3
```

```
window 6
```

```
defenestrate 12
```

Code that adjusts an assortment while repeating over that equivalent assortment can be precarious to get right. Rather, it is normally increasingly straight-forward to circle over a duplicate of the assortment or to make another assortment:

```
# Strategy: Iterate over a duplicate
```

```
for client, status in users.copy().items():
```

```
on the off chance that status == 'idle':
```

```
del users[user]
```

```
# Strategy: Create another assortment
```

```
active_users = {}
```

for client, status in users.items():

on the off chance that status == 'dynamic':

active_users[user] = status

4.3. The range() Function

On the off chance that you do need to repeat over a grouping of numbers, the implicit capacity extend() proves to be useful. It produces number juggling movements:

```
>>>
```

```
>>> for I in range(5):

... print(i)
```

...

0

1

2

3

4

The given end point is never part of the produced
succession; range(10) creates 10 qualities, the lawful files
for things of an arrangement of length 10. It is conceivable
to let the range start at another number, or to determine an
alternate augmentation (even negative; some of the time
this is known as the 'progression'):

range(5, 10)

5, 6, 7, 8, 9

range(0, 10, 3)

0, 3, 6, 9

run(- 10, - 100, - 30)

- 10, - 40, - 70

To emphasize over the lists of a succession, you can consolidate go() and len() as pursues:

>>>

>>> a = ['Mary', 'had', 'a', 'bit', 'lamb']

```
>>> for I in range(len(a)):

... print(i, a[i])

...

0 Mary

1 had

2 a

3 little

4 sheep
```

In most such cases, be that as it may, it is helpful to utilize the identify() work, see Looping Techniques.

A bizarre thing occurs in the event that you simply print a range:

```
>>>
```

```
>>> print(range(10))
```

```
range(0, 10)
```

From multiple points of view the item returned by run() acts as though it is a rundown, yet in truth it isn't. It is an article which restores the progressive things of the ideal succession when you emphasize over it, however it doesn't generally make the rundown, in this way sparing space.

We state such an article is iterable, that is, reasonable as an objective for capacities and builds that expect something from which they can get progressive things until the stockpile is depleted. We have seen that the for proclamation is such a build, while a case of capacity that takes an iterable is aggregate():

```
>>>
```

```
>>> sum(range(4)) # 0 + 1 + 2 + 3
```

6

Later we will see more capacities that arrival iterables and take iterables as contentions. Finally, perhaps you are interested about how to get a rundown from a range. Here is the arrangement:

```
>>>
```

```
>>> list(range(4))
```

[0, 1, 2, 3]

In section Data Structures, we will talk about in more insight regarding list().

4.4. break and proceed with Statements, and else Clauses on Loops

The break articulation, as in C, breaks out of the deepest encasing for or while circle.

Circle articulations may have an else provision; it is executed when the circle ends through weariness of the iterable (with for) or when the condition turns out to be bogus (with while), however not when the circle is ended by a break explanation. This is exemplified by the accompanying circle, which looks for prime numbers:

>>>

```
>>> for n in range(2, 10):
... for x in range(2, n):
... in the event that n % x == 0:
... print(n, 'approaches', x, '*', n//x)
... break
... else:
... # circle fell through without finding a factor
... print(n, 'is a prime number')
...
```

2 is a prime number

3 is a prime number

4 equivalents 2 * 2

5 is a prime number

6 equivalents 2 * 3

7 is a prime number

8 equivalents 2 * 4

9 equivalents 3 * 3

(Truly, this is the right code. Look carefully: the else proviso has a place with the for circle, not the if proclamation.)

At the point when utilized with a circle, the else proviso shares more for all intents and purpose with the else condition of an attempt proclamation than it does with that of if articulations: an attempt explanation's else statement runs when no exemption happens, and a circle's else proviso runs when no break happens. For additional on the attempt proclamation and special cases, see Handling Exceptions.

The proceed with explanation, likewise obtained from C, proceeds with the following emphasis of the circle:

>>>

>>> for num in range(2, 10):

... on the off chance that num % 2 == 0:

... print("Found a significantly number", num)

... proceed

... print("Found a number", num)

Discovered a significantly number 2

Discovered a number 3

Discovered a significantly number 4

Discovered a number 5

Discovered a significantly number 6

Discovered a number 7

Discovered a significantly number 8

Discovered a number 9

4.5. pass Statements

The pass explanation sits idle. It very well may be utilized when an announcement is required grammatically yet the program requires no activity. For instance:

```
>>>
```

```
>>> while True:
```

```
... pass # Busy-sit tight for console intrude on (Ctrl+C)
```

...

This is regularly utilized for making insignificant classes:

>>>

>>> class MyEmptyClass:

... pass

...

Somewhere else pass can be utilized is as a spot holder for a capacity or contingent body when you are taking a shot at new code, enabling you to continue thinking at a progressively unique level. The pass is quietly overlooked:

>>>

```
>>> def initlog(*args):
```

```
... pass # Remember to execute this!
```

```
...
```

4.6. Characterizing Functions

We can make a capacity that composes the Fibonacci arrangement to a subjective limit:

```
>>>
```

```
>>> def fib(n): # compose Fibonacci arrangement up to n
```

```
... """Print a Fibonacci arrangement up to n."""
```

```
... a, b = 0, 1
```

```
... while a < n:
... print(a, end=' ')
... a, b = b, a+b
... print()
...
>>> # Now call the capacity we simply characterized:
... fib(2000)
0 1 2 3 5 8 13 21 34 55 89 144 233 377 610 987 1597
```

The watchword def presents a capacity definition. It must be trailed by the capacity name and the parenthesized rundown of formal parameters. The explanations that structure the body of the capacity start at the following line, and should be indented.

The principal articulation of the capacity body can alternatively be a string exacting; this string strict is the capacity's documentation string, or docstring. (Progressively about docstrings can be found in the area Documentation Strings.) There are apparatuses which use docstrings to consequently create on the web or printed documentation, or to let the client intuitively peruse through code; it's great practice to incorporate docstrings in code that you compose, so make a propensity for it.

Chapter 7

Class and Objects in Python

Classes and Objects

Articles are an epitome of factors and capacities into a solitary element. Articles get their factors and capacities from classes. Classes are basically a format to make your articles.

An extremely fundamental class would look something like this:

script.py

IPython Shell

Run

Controlled by DataCamp

We'll disclose why you need to incorporate that "self" as a parameter somewhat later. To start with, to dole out the above class(template) to an item you would do the accompanying:

script.py

IPython Shell

Run

Fueled by DataCamp

Presently the variable "myobjectx" holds an object of the class "MyClass" that contains the variable and the capacity characterized inside the class called "MyClass".

Getting to Object Variables

To get to the variable within the recently made article "myobjectx" you would do the accompanying:

script.py

IPython Shell

Run

Controlled by DataCamp

So for example the beneath would yield the string "blah":

script.py

IPython Shell

Run

Controlled by DataCamp

You can make numerous various articles that are of the equivalent class(have similar factors and capacities characterized). Be that as it may, each article contains free duplicates of the factors characterized in the class. For example, if we somehow happened to characterize another item with the "MyClass" class and afterward change the string in the variable above:

script.py

IPython Shell

Run

Fueled by DataCamp

Getting to Object Functions

To get to a capacity within an item you use documentation like getting to a variable:

script.py

IPython Shell

Run

Controlled by DataCamp

The above would print out the message, "This is a message inside the class."

Exercise

We have a class characterized for vehicles. Make two new vehicles called car1 and car2. Set car1 to be a red convertible worth $60,000.00 with a name of Fer, and car2 to be a blue van named Jump worth $10,000.00.

script.py

Chapter 8

Data and Time

In Python, date, time and datetime classes gives various capacity to manage dates, times and time interims. Date and datetime are an article in Python, so when you control them, you are really controlling items and not string or timestamps. At whatever point you control dates or time, you have to import datetime work.

The datetime classes in Python are ordered into primary 5 classes.

date – Manipulate simply date (Month, day, year)

time – Time autonomous of the day (Hour, minute, second, microsecond)

datetime – Combination of time and date (Month, day, year, hour, second, microsecond) timedelta—A length of time utilized for controlling dates

tzinfo—A theoretical class for managing time zones

In this instructional exercise, we will learn-

The most effective method to Use Date and DateTime Class

Print Date utilizing date.today()

Python Current Date and Time: presently() today()

The most effective method to Format Date and Time Output with Strftime()

The most effective method to utilize Timedelta Objects

The most effective method to Use Date and DateTime Class

Stage 1) Before you run the code for datetime, it is significant that you import the date time modules as appeared in the screen capture beneath.

Python Date and Time Tutorial: Timedelta, Datetime, and Strftime

These import articulations are pre-characterized bits of usefulness in the Python library that let you controls dates and times, without composing any code.

Consider the accompanying focuses before executing the datetime code

from datetime import date

This line tells the Python translator that from the datetime module import the date class We are not composing the code for this date usefulness oh dear simply bringing in it for our utilization

Stage 2) Next, we make an occurrence of the date object.

Python Date and Time Tutorial: Timedelta, Datetime, and Strftime

Stage 3) Next, we print the date and run the code.

Python Date and Time Tutorial: Timedelta, Datetime, and Strftime

The yield is true to form.

Print Date utilizing date.today()

date.today work has a few properties related with it. We can print singular day/month/year and numerous different things

We should see a model

Python Date and Time Tutorial: Timedelta, Datetime, and Strftime

The present Weekday Number

The date.today() work likewise gives you the weekday number. Here is the Weekday Table which start with Monday as 0 and Sunday as 6

Day

WeekDay Number

Monday

0

Tuesday

1

Wednesday

2

Thursday

3

Friday

4

Saturday

5

Sunday

6

Weekday Number is valuable for exhibits whose list is subject to the Day of the week.

Python Date and Time Tutorial: Timedelta, Datetime, and Strftime

Python Current Date and Time: presently() today()

Stage 1) Like Date Objects, we can likewise utilize "DATETIME OBJECTS" in Python. It gives date alongside time in hours, minutes, seconds and milliseconds.

Python Date and Time Tutorial: Timedelta, Datetime, and Strftime

At the point when we execute the code for datetime, it gives the yield with current date and time.

Stage 2) With "DATETIME OBJECT", you can likewise call time class.

Assume we need to print only the present time without the date.

t = datetime.time(datetime.now())

We had imported the time class. We will dole out it the present estimation of time utilizing datetime.now()

We are allotting the estimation of the present time to the variable t.

Chapter 9

Advanced Features, Data analysis and Features

5 Advanced Features of Python and How to Use Them

George Seif

Python is an excellent language. Easy to utilize yet effectively expressive. In any case, would you say you are utilizing everything that it brings to the table?

The propelled highlights of any programming language are generally found through broad experience. You're coding up a muddled task and wind up scanning for something on stackoverflow. You at that point go over a wonderfully rich answer for your concern that uses a Python include you never at any point knew existed!

That is absolutely the funnest approach to learn: disclosure by investigation and mishap!

Here are 5 of the most valuable propelled highlights of the Python programming language — and all the more critically how to utilize them!

(1) Lambda capacities

A Lambda Function is a little, mysterious capacity — unknown as in it doesn't really have a name.

Python capacities are commonly characterized utilizing the style of def a_function_name() , however with lambda capacities we don't give it a name by any stretch of the imagination. We do this on the grounds that the reason for a lambda work is to play out some sort of straightforward articulation or activity without the requirement for completely characterizing a capacity.

A lambda capacity can take any number of contentions, yet should consistently have just a single articulation:

Perceive how simple that was! We played out a touch of essential math without the requirement for characterizing an all out capacity. This is one of the numerous highlights of Python that makes it a spotless and oversimplified programming language to utilize.

(2) Maps

Guide() is a worked in Python work used to apply a capacity to a grouping of components like a rundown or word reference. It's a perfect and in particular comprehensible manner to perform such an activity.

Look at the model above! We can apply our capacity to a solitary rundown or various records. Actually, you can utilize a guide with any python work you can consider, as long as it's good with the arrangement components you are working on.

(3) Filtering

The Filter worked in work is very like the Map work in that it applies a capacity to a grouping (list, tuple, word reference). The key distinction is that channel() will just restore the components which the applied capacity returned as True.

Look at the model beneath for a representation:

In addition to the fact that we evaluated True or False for each rundown component, the channel() work likewise tried to just restore the components which coordinated as True. Extremely helpful for taking care of to two stages of checking an articulation and building an arrival list.

(4) Itertools

The Python Itertools module is an assortment of apparatuses for dealing with iterators. An iterator is an information type that can be utilized in a for circle including records, tuples, and word references.

Utilizing the capacities in the Itertools module will enable you to perform numerous iterator tasks that would regularly require multi-line works and confounded rundown appreciation. Look at the models beneath for a great delineation of the enchantment of Itertools!

(5) Generators

Generator capacities enable you to pronounce a capacity that carries on like an iterator, for example it very well may be utilized in a for circle. This significantly disentangles your code and is substantially more memory productive than a straightforward for circle.

Chapter 10

Files in Python

Python File Handling: Create, Open, Append, Read, Write

In Python, there is no requirement for bringing in outer library to peruse and compose documents. Python gives an inbuilt capacity to making, composing and understanding documents.

In this instructional exercise, we will learn

The most effective method to Create a Text File

The most effective method to Append Data to a File

The most effective method to Read a File

The most effective method to Read a File line by line

Document Modes in Python

The most effective method to Create a Text File

With Python you can make a .content documents
(guru99.txt) by utilizing the code, we have shown here how
you can do this

Stage 1)

f= open("guru99.txt","w+")

We pronounced the variable f to open a record named
textfile.txt. Open takes 2 contentions, the document that we
need to open and a string that speaks to the sorts of consent
or activity we need to do on the record

Here we utilized "w" letter in our contention, which
demonstrates compose and the in addition to sign that

implies it will make a record in the event that it doesn't exist in library

Additionally sign methods, on the off chance that File isn't there, at that point make it

The accessible alternative adjacent to "w" are, "r" for read, and "a" for annex

Stage 2)

for I in range(10):

f.write("This is line %d\r\n" % (i+1))

We have a for circle that runs over a scope of 10 numbers.

Utilizing the compose capacity to enter information into the document.

The yield we need to repeat in the document is "this is line number", which we proclaim with compose capacity and afterward percent d (shows whole number)

So fundamentally we are placing in the line number that we are composing, at that point placing it in a carriage return and another line character

Stage 3)

f.close()

This will close the example of the document guru99.txt put away

Here is the outcome after code execution

Python FILE Tutorial: Create, Append, Read, Write

At the point when you click on your content document for our situation "guru99.txt" it will look something like this

Python FILE Tutorial: Create, Append, Read, Write

Step by step instructions to Append Data to a File

You can likewise attach another content to the previously existing document or the new record.

Stage 1)

```
f=open("guru99.txt", "a+")
```

By and by on the off chance that you could see an or more sign in the code, it shows that it will make another record on the off chance that it doesn't exist. Yet, for our situation we as of now have the document, so we are not required to make another record.

Stage 2)

```python
for I in range(2):
```

```python
f.write("Appended line %d\r\n" % (i+1))
```

This will compose information into the document in attach mode.

Python FILE Tutorial: Create, Append, Read, Write

You can see the yield in "guru99.txt" document. The yield of the code is that prior record is annexed with new information.

Step by step instructions to Read a File

Not just you can make .txt document from Python yet you can likewise call .txt record in a "read mode"(r).

Stage 1) Open the record in Read mode

f=open("guru99.txt", "r")

Stage 2) We utilize the mode work in the code to watch that the record is in open mode. In the event that indeed, we continue ahead

on the off chance that f.mode == 'r':

Stage 3) Use f.read to peruse record information and store it in factor content substance =f.read()

Stage 4) print substance

Here is the yield

Python FILE Tutorial: Create, Append, Read, Write

The most effective method to Read a File line by line

You can likewise peruse your .txt document line by line if your information is too huge to peruse. This code will isolate your information in simple to prepared mode

Python FILE Tutorial: Create, Append, Read, Write

At the point when you run the code (f1=f.readlines()) for perusing the record or archive line by line, it will isolate each line and present the document in a decipherable arrangement. For our situation the line is short and intelligible, the yield will seem to be like the read mode. In any case, if there is a perplexing information record which isn't decipherable, this bit of code could be valuable.

Chapter 11

Machine Learning

Your First Machine Learning Project in Python Step-By-Step

Would you like to do AI utilizing Python, yet you're experiencing difficulty beginning?

In this post, you will finish your first AI venture utilizing Python.

In this bit by bit instructional exercise you will:

Download and introduce Python SciPy and get the most helpful bundle for AI in Python.

Burden a dataset and comprehend it's structure utilizing measurable rundowns and information perception.

Make 6 AI models, pick the best and fabricate certainty that the exactness is dependable.

In the event that you are an AI novice and looking to at long last begin utilizing Python, this instructional exercise was intended for you.

Find how to get ready information with pandas, fit and assess models with scikit-learn, and more in my new book, with 16 bit by bit instructional exercises, 3 activities, and full python code.

We should begin!

Update Jan/2017: Updated to reflect changes to the scikit-learn API in adaptation 0.18.

Update Mar/2017: Added connections to help arrangement your Python condition.

Update Apr/2018: Added some accommodating connections about arbitrariness and making forecasts.

Update Sep/2018: Added connection to my very own facilitated variant of the dataset as UCI has gotten inconsistent.

Update Feb/2019: Updated to address alerts with sklearn API rendition 0.20+ with SVM and Logistic Regression, likewise refreshed outcomes and plots.

Update Oct/2019: Added joins toward the conclusion to extra instructional exercises to progress forward.

Update Nov/2019: Added full code models for each area.

Your First Machine Learning Project in Python Step-By-Step

Your First Machine Learning Project in Python Step-By-Step

Photograph by cosmoflash, a few rights held.

How Do You Start Machine Learning in Python?

The most ideal approach to learn AI is by structuring and finishing little undertakings.

Python Can Be Intimidating When Getting Started

Python is a well known and amazing deciphered language. In contrast to R, Python is a finished language and stage that you can use for both innovative work and creating generation frameworks.

There are likewise a great deal of modules and libraries to look over, giving various approaches to carry out every responsibility. It can feel overpowering.

The most ideal approach to begin utilizing Python for AI is to finished a venture.

It will constrain you to introduce and begin the Python translator (at any rate).

It will given you a superior perspective on the most proficient method to step through a little venture.

It will give you certainty, possibly to go without anyone else little activities.

Learners Need A Small End-to-End Project

Books and courses are baffling. They give you heaps of plans and bits, however you never get the opportunity to perceive how they all fit together.

At the point when you are applying AI to your very own datasets, you are taking a shot at a venture.

An AI undertaking may not be straight, yet it has various surely understood advances:

Characterize Problem.

Plan Data.

Assess Algorithms.

Improve Results.

Present Results.

The most ideal approach to truly grapple with another stage or device is to work through an AI venture start to finish and cover the key advances. To be specific, from stacking information, outlining information, assessing calculations and making a few expectations.

On the off chance that you can do that, you have a layout that you can use on dataset after dataset. You can fill in the holes, for example, further information arrangement and improving outcome assignments later, when you have more certainty.

Hi World of Machine Learning

The best little undertaking to begin with on another apparatus is the arrangement of iris blossoms (for example the iris dataset).

This is a decent venture since it is so surely known.

Traits are numeric so you need to make sense of how to load and deal with information.

It is an arrangement issue, enabling you to rehearse with maybe a simpler sort of regulated learning calculation.

It is a multi-class grouping issue (multi-ostensible) that may require some particular taking care of.

It just has 4 properties and 150 columns, which means it is little and effectively fits into memory (and a screen or A4 page).

The entirety of the numeric qualities are in similar units and a similar scale, not requiring any extraordinary scaling or changes to begin.

How about we begin with your welcome world AI venture in Python.

AI in Python: Step-By-Step Tutorial

(start here)

In this area, we are getting down to business through a little AI venture start to finish.

Here is a diagram of what we are going to cover:

Introducing the Python and SciPy stage.

Stacking the dataset.

Condensing the dataset.

Imagining the dataset.

Assessing a few calculations.

Making a few expectations.

Take as much time as necessary. Work through each progression.

Attempt to type in the directions yourself or reorder the directions to speed things up.

On the off chance that you have any inquiries whatsoever, it would be ideal if you leave a remark at the base of the post.

Need assistance with Machine Learning in Python?

Take my free 2-week email course and find information prep, calculations and that's only the tip of the iceberg (with code).

Snap to join now and furthermore get a free PDF Ebook form of the course.

Start Your FREE Mini-Course Now!

1. Downloading, Installing and Starting Python SciPy

Get the Python and SciPy stage introduced on your framework on the off chance that it isn't as of now.

I would prefer not to cover this in incredible detail, since others as of now have. This is as of now entirely direct, particularly in the event that you are an engineer. On the off chance that you do require help, pose an inquiry in the remarks.

1.1 Install SciPy Libraries

This instructional exercise accept Python form 2.7 or 3.6+.

There are 5 key libraries that you should introduce. The following is a rundown of the Python SciPy libraries required for this instructional exercise:

scipy

numpy

matplotlib

pandas

sklearn

There are numerous approaches to introduce these libraries. My best counsel is to pick one technique at that point be reliable in introducing every library.

1. Downloading, Installing and Starting Python SciPy

Get the Python and SciPy stage introduced on your framework on the off chance that it isn't as of now.

I would prefer not to cover this in extraordinary detail, since others as of now have. This is as of now quite clear, particularly on the off chance that you are a designer. In the event that you do require help, pose an inquiry in the remarks.

1.1 Install SciPy Libraries

This instructional exercise accept Python rendition 2.7 or 3.6+.

There are 5 key libraries that you should introduce. The following is a rundown of the Python SciPy libraries required for this instructional exercise:

scipy

numpy

matplotlib

pandas

sklearn

There are numerous approaches to introduce these libraries. My best guidance is to pick one strategy at that point be reliable in introducing every library.

The scipy establishment page gives amazing guidelines to introducing the above libraries on various stages, for example, Linux, macintosh OS X and Windows. In the event that you have any questions or questions, allude to this guide, it has been trailed by a great many individuals.

On Mac OS X, you can utilize macports to introduce Python 3.6 and these libraries. For more data on macports, see the landing page.

On Linux you can utilize your bundle director, for example, yum on Fedora to introduce RPMs.

On the off chance that you are on Windows or you are not certain, I would suggest introducing the free form of Anaconda that incorporates all that you need.

Note: This instructional exercise accept you have scikit-learn form 0.20 or higher introduced.

Need more help? See one of these instructional exercises:

The most effective method to Setup a Python Environment for Machine Learning with Anaconda

The most effective method to Create a Linux Virtual Machine For Machine Learning With Python 3

1.2 Start Python and Check Versions

It is a smart thought to ensure your Python condition was introduced effectively and is functioning true to form.

The content underneath will assist you with testing out your condition. It imports every library required in this instructional exercise and prints the adaptation.

Open a direction line and start the python translator:

python

1

python

I suggest working straightforwardly in the mediator or composing your contents and running them on the direction line instead of enormous editors and IDEs. Keep things basic and spotlight on the AI not the toolchain.

Type or reorder the accompanying content:

```python
# Check the variants of libraries

# Python adaptation

import sys

print('Python: {}'.format(sys.version))

# scipy

import scipy

print('scipy: {}'.format(scipy._version_))

# numpy

import numpy
```

```python
print('numpy: {}'.format(numpy._version_))

# matplotlib

import matplotlib

print('matplotlib: {}'.format(matplotlib._version_))

# pandas

import pandas

print('pandas: {}'.format(pandas._version_))

# scikit-learn

import sklearn
```

```
print('sklearn: {}'.format(sklearn._version_))
```

1

2

3

4

5

6

7

8

9

10

11

12

13

14

15

16

17

18

19

20

Check the adaptations of libraries

Python adaptation

import sys

print('Python: {}'.format(sys.version))

scipy

import scipy

```python
print('scipy: {}'.format(scipy._version_))

# numpy

import numpy

print('numpy: {}'.format(numpy._version_))

# matplotlib

import matplotlib

print('matplotlib: {}'.format(matplotlib._version_))

# pandas

import pandas
```

```
print('pandas: {}'.format(pandas._version_))
```

```
# scikit-learn
```

```
import sklearn
```

```
print('sklearn: {}'.format(sklearn._version_))
```

Here is the yield I jump on my OS X workstation:

```
Python: 3.6.9 (default, Oct 19 2019, 05:21:45)
```

```
[GCC 4.2.1 Compatible Apple LLVM 9.1.0 (crash
902.0.39.2)]
```

```
scipy: 1.3.1
```

numpy: 1.17.3

matplotlib: 3.1.1

pandas: 0.25.1

sklearn: 0.21.3

1

2

3

4

5

6

7

Python: 3.6.9 (default, Oct 19 2019, 05:21:45)

[GCC 4.2.1 Compatible Apple LLVM 9.1.0 (crash 902.0.39.2)]

scipy: 1.3.1

numpy: 1.17.3

matplotlib: 3.1.1

pandas: 0.25.1

sklearn: 0.21.3

Contrast the above yield with your adaptations.

In a perfect world, your renditions should coordinate or be later. The APIs don't change rapidly, so don't be excessively concerned in the event that you are a couple of renditions behind, Everything in this instructional exercise will probably still work for you.

In the event that you get a blunder, stop. Right now is an ideal opportunity to fix it.

In the event that you can't run the above content neatly you won't have the option to finish this instructional exercise.

My best guidance is to Google look for your mistake message or post an inquiry on Stack Exchange.

2. Burden The Data

We are going to utilize the iris blooms dataset. This dataset is well known in light of the fact that it is utilized as the "welcome world" dataset in AI and measurements by basically everybody.

The dataset contains 150 perceptions of iris blooms. There are four sections of estimations of the blooms in centimeters. The fifth segment is the types of the blossom watched. Every single watched blossom have a place with one of three animal groups.

You can become familiar with this dataset on Wikipedia.

In this progression we are going to stack the iris information from CSV record URL.

2.1 Import libraries

To start with, how about we import the entirety of the modules, capacities and articles we are going to use in this instructional exercise.

Load libraries

from pandas import read_csv

from pandas.plotting import scatter_matrix

from matplotlib import pyplot

from sklearn.model_selection import train_test_split

from sklearn.model_selection import cross_val_score

from sklearn.model_selection import StratifiedKFold

```python
from sklearn.metrics import classification_report

from sklearn.metrics import confusion_matrix

from sklearn.metrics import accuracy_score

from sklearn.linear_model import LogisticRegression

from sklearn.tree import DecisionTreeClassifier

from sklearn.neighbors import KNeighborsClassifier

from sklearn.discriminant_analysis import
LinearDiscriminantAnalysis

from sklearn.naive_bayes import GaussianNB
```

from sklearn.svm import SVC

1

2

3

4

5

6

7

8

9

10

11

12

13

14

15

16

Load libraries

```python
from pandas import read_csv
```

267

```python
from pandas.plotting import scatter_matrix
```

```python
from matplotlib import pyplot
```

```python
from sklearn.model_selection import train_test_split
```

```python
from sklearn.model_selection import cross_val_score
```

```python
from sklearn.model_selection import StratifiedKFold
```

```python
from sklearn.metrics import classification_report
```

```python
from sklearn.metrics import confusion_matrix
```

```python
from sklearn.metrics import accuracy_score
```

from sklearn.linear_model import LogisticRegression

from sklearn.tree import DecisionTreeClassifier

from sklearn.neighbors import KNeighborsClassifier

from sklearn.discriminant_analysis import
LinearDiscriminantAnalysis

from sklearn.naive_bayes import GaussianNB

from sklearn.svm import SVC

Everything should stack without blunder. On the off chance that you have a mistake, stop. You need a working SciPy condition before proceeding. See the guidance above about setting up your condition.

2.2 Load Dataset

We can stack the information legitimately from the UCI Machine Learning storehouse.

We are utilizing pandas to stack the information. We will likewise utilize pandas beside investigate the information both with elucidating measurements and information representation.

Note that we are indicating the names of every section when stacking the information. This will help later when we investigate the information.

\# Load dataset

url = "https://raw.githubusercontent.com/jbrownlee/Datasets/ace/iris.csv"

names = ['sepal-length', 'sepal-width', 'petal-length', 'petal-width', 'class']

dataset = read_csv(url, names=names)

1

2

3

4

Load dataset

url = "https://raw.githubusercontent.com/jbrownlee/Datasets/ace/iris.csv"

names = ['sepal-length', 'sepal-width', 'petal-length', 'petal-width', 'class']

dataset = read_csv(url, names=names)

The dataset should stack without episode.

On the off chance that you do have organize issues, you can download the iris.csv document into your working registry and burden it utilizing a similar strategy, changing URL to the nearby record name.

3. Outline the Dataset

Presently the time has come to investigate the information.

In this progression we are going to investigate the information a couple of various ways:

Measurements of the dataset.

Look at the information itself.

Measurable synopsis everything being equal.

Breakdown of the information by the class variable.

Try not to stress, each take a gander at the information is one direction. These are helpful directions that you can utilize over and over on future activities.

3.1 Dimensions of Dataset

We can get a fast thought of what number of cases (lines) and what number of properties (sections) the information contains with the shape property.

```
# shape
```

```
print(dataset.shape)
```

1

2

```
# shape
```

```
print(dataset.shape)
```

You should see 150 occasions and 5 properties:

```
(150, 5)
```

1

(150, 5)

3.2 Peek at the Data

It is likewise constantly a smart thought to really eyeball your information.

head

print(dataset.head(20))

1

2

head

print(dataset.head(20))

You should see the initial 20 columns of the information:

sepal-length sepal-width petal-length petal-width class

0 5.1 3.5 1.4 0.2 Iris-setosa

1 4.9 3.0 1.4 0.2 Iris-setosa

2 4.7 3.2 1.3 0.2 Iris-setosa

3 4.6 3.1 1.5 0.2 Iris-setosa

4 5.0 3.6 1.4 0.2 Iris-setosa

5 5.4 3.9 1.7 0.4 Iris-setosa

6 4.6 3.4 1.4 0.3 Iris-setosa

7 5.0 3.4 1.5 0.2 Iris-setosa

8 4.4 2.9 1.4 0.2 Iris-setosa

9 4.9 3.1 1.5 0.1 Iris-setosa

10 5.4 3.7 1.5 0.2 Iris-setosa

11 4.8 3.4 1.6 0.2 Iris-setosa

12 4.8 3.0 1.4 0.1 Iris-setosa

13 4.3 3.0 1.1 0.1 Iris-setosa

14 5.8 4.0 1.2 0.2 Iris-setosa

15 5.7 4.4 1.5 0.4 Iris-setosa

16 5.4 3.9 1.3 0.4 Iris-setosa

17 5.1 3.5 1.4 0.3 Iris-setosa

18 5.7 3.8 1.7

Conclusion

By and large, the progressions sketched out here have a high effect as far as updates required to the mediator, however shouldn't profoundly change the manner by which you compose your Python code. It's a matter of propensity, for example, utilizing enclosures with print—or rather, print(). When you have these progressions added to your repertoire, you're well on your approach to having the option to hop to the new stage. It possibly somewhat surprising from the start, yet it's a change that has been desiring some time. Try not to freeze; 2.x will live on for quite a while to come. The change will be moderate, purposeful, torment safe, and even-keeled. Welcome to the beginning of the people to come!

www.ingramcontent.com/pod-product-compliance
Lightning Source LLC
LaVergne TN
LVHW020048210726
843507LV00015B/12